TIME
to FLY

TIME to FLY

Life and Love after Loss

Eileen Robertson Hamra

CITY POINT PRESS

WESTPORT

Quoted lyrics from:

"We Live on Borrowed Time," written by David Allen Friedman, published by Midder Music
Publishing, Inc. © Midder Music Publishing, Inc.

"Live Like We're Dying," by Steve Kipner, Andrew Frampton, Mark Anthony Sheehan, Daniel
John O'Donoghue, © Universal Music-Z Tunes, EMI April Music, Inc., Sonic Graffiti, EMI
Music Publishing, Ltd., EMI Blackwood Music, Inc., OBO EMI Music Publishing, Ltd.

"You and Me," written by David John Matthews © Colden Grey, Ltd.

City Point Press
P.O. Box 2063
Westport CT 06880
www.citypointpress.com

Distributed worldwide by Simon and Schuster

Paperback ISBN 978-1-947951-18-1
eBook ISBN 978-1-947951-19-8

Cover by Ann Weinstock
Book design by Barbara Aronica-Buck

Second printing, July, 2020

Manufactured in Canada

For Melanie, Brooke, Max, and Zack.

A wise person once told me that your children are your most important spiritual guides. I have found that to be unquestionably true. I am a much better human because I share my life with you. Thank you for constantly teaching me to be patient, to question what I know, to forgive myself and others, to take risks, and to have fun and play. I love you more than you know, and this book is for you.

Acknowledgments

Time to Fly would not be in your hands if it were not for the guidance, brilliance, and hard work of Christine Fadden. Thank you, Christine, for being my copilot in bringing this book to life. I brought my story and you brought your talent, and together we've created a book that I hope will make a difference for whoever reads it. You are a writing goddess, and I feel immensely blessed to have found and worked with you.

This book would also not have been possible if it were not for the unconditional loving support of my sister Mary Kay. No one on the planet knows me better and still loves me more than you do. Thank you for your unrelenting encouragement, which has given me the strength to be vulnerable and share my story.

I want to thank my husbands, Brian and Mike. It is still unbelievable to me that I was lucky enough to meet two amazing men brave enough to love me the way you both have. It may be weird to thank two husbands, but that's the way life turned out for me, and making one more important than the other would be inauthentic. I do, however, want to especially acknowledge Mike for not only loving and supporting me in everything I do, but also stepping in and up to be the most amazing dad to all of our children. I adore and admire your endless patience, love, and commitment for our family.

I have immense gratitude for my parents, who taught me to love and to value family. Mom and Dad, you were unwavering role models for overcoming loss, and I know how lucky I am to have you both.

To the rest of my family, whether we are related by blood or marriage, who are named or referred to in the book, thank you for being the people you are so that I could write authentically about each of you and be proud to call you family.

I would also like to thank all of the amazing people in my life without whom I would not have the stories I share in this book. I wish I could have included all of our stories, but a book has to end somewhere. However, I want the world to know how important you've been in my family's life. Thank you to Roxanne Betz, Marcia Colendar, Ann Ostapovicz, Ronda Sharman, Gina Peters, Kendra Gray, Erin Doyle, Joe and Dan Settineri-Ross, Rhaea Dautel, Julie Frisch, Erin Walker, Andy Rogovin, Monique Byrne, Patrick Corbett, Bob Mason, Megan Weeks, Frank and Kerty Levy, Jay and Larissa Henderson, Brian and Heather Kennealy, Walter and Sengdara Vonkoch, Fred and Becky Ackerman, Jen and Matt Edstrom, Ken Dinovo, and Lajung Lee, Shane and Anna Crotty, Lisa and Theo Schlossnagle, Hillary and Charlie Kunda, Marty Cowan, Kara Atkinson, Emily Higgins, Stephanie and Rob Glenn, Julie Reisler, Julie Philips, Kim Morrison, Suzanne Simpson, Jessica Eustace, Kaliopi Polizos, Tracey Dowden, Sharon Ritter, Nikki Gordon Hylinski, Kelly Meissner, Alicyn Mullins, Missy and Greg Weiss, Anna Bazalar, Lisa Sandler, Wally King, Stephanie Mondino, Janet Littlejohn, Monica Carroll, Kathleen Sand, Heather Peterson, Red Jen Ford,

Mary and Paul LaBahn, Linda and Bob Axel, Carol delaTorre, Debbie delaCuesta, Heather Lambert, Deborah Wallin, Karishma Shaw, Radhika Seneviratne, Bivian Rodriguez, Beverly Skytte, Loretta Martinez, Janis Candelaria, Marci Turner, May Kaplan, Carol Colshan, Dan and Stephanie Kippen, Todd Jardine, Eric Brooks, Tommy and Debbie Iorio, Becky and Paul Kirby, Jillian and John Kamps, Bob and Kathy Saurman, Kelly and Rusty Eddy, Bruce and Debbie Galien, Manuel and Lulu Estrada, Andrew Keyt, Lou and Emily Yaffe, Edie Milosevic, Melissa Chrusfield, Jennifer Tengelsen, Tiffany Miller Spriggs, Leslee Patras, Erica Holman, Kimberly Steinbeck, Dr. Angeline Beltsos and her staff, Stephanie Hannon, Dan Gertsacov, Tom Vanden Bussche and Deborah Loones, Claire Broido Johnson, Jigar Shah, Tran Luu, Adam Plesniak, Yolanda Seabrooks, Paul and Karen Lightfoot, Guy Blanchard, Jason Bohle, Bob and Sharon Mueller, Angela Boyd, Marci and Craig Willems, Helen Gilhooly, Tobin White, Toni Kendall, Carol Tisson, Sarah Culberson, Carolyn Fine, Jill Derby, Christina Rasmussen, Carolyn Agnew, Lindsey Avner, Amy Farbman, Megan Hoffman, Carrie Hutchinson, Justine Whiteside, Lindsey Ruder, Molly Owens, Lindsey Ross, Brynn Rosner, Edith Small, Kristi Kedrick and Tiani Pagan.

Thank you to all the writing and publishing professionals who have worked with me throughout the years on getting this book published: Lindsey Smith, Christine Kloser, Kim Morrison, Adam Gamble, Mary Bisbee-Beek, David Wilk, Ann Weinstock, and Kitty Burns Florey.

Preface

I have learned many things over the seven years since my husband's death, and many more since my younger sister's death two decades ago. Primary among these lessons is that it is possible to turn tragedy into a gift. It is possible to use pain as a transformational guide. And it is possible that the life you create after you move through the darkest days of your life will be brighter than you ever could have imagined.

Passing through darkness, though, always reminds me of the refrain of the famous children's book by Michael Rosen, *We're Going on a Bear Hunt*: "We can't go over it. We can't go under it. OH NO! We've got to go through it!"

The willingness to go through it—whatever "it" is—is what makes for a great life. This book is about my journey through it.

I know that life and our experience of it occurs differently for everyone. In the book, I share as truthful a perspective and representation as I can offer about the people in my life that I know and love. They are journeying with me, and witnessing their best and worst days has impacted me in profound ways. This book is testament to my fortune in the family and friends I have.

In the health and healing workshops and networks I have engaged in over the course of my adult life, whether to press through my own doubts and perceived limitations, or to process my own grief and learn how to understand the grief of my children in its many acute, indirect, and delayed manifestations, I have encountered so many people whose decades-old loss is as fresh for them now as it was the day the dreaded call came. Or the late-night knock on the door. Or the helicopter circling overhead, just past the small York County Airport landing strip, where plane N48BS was supposed to have taxied and then parked. Where Brian was supposed to disembark, arms full of Christmas gifts.

My hope is that this book, this story, meets you wherever you are in your journey, whether you are deep in some sort of complex struggle, or emerging into a newfound light.

This book is my story, and I will be turning its pages far beyond the last page you turn here. If something calls to you or stays with you—be it some spirit of the people still alive or the spirits of my sister and Brian, who may be physically gone but still present in many ways—whatever may be of help here is yours for the taking.

Please know that in the dark that follows loss, having been given permission to be exactly who I am, and to fully experience what was happening at the time it was happening, has been nothing short of illuminating. The family I was raised in, the family I have made with the two loves of my life, and the tribe I have in friendship are gifts. I wish for you the same.

Prologue

Brooke Robertson
8th Grade Language and Literature

12-22-11

12-1-17. 24 more days until Christmas. 21 until it is 6 years since he departed. Christmas always brings spirits of joy. Christmas brings family together. 6 years ago, my father's plane was torn from the sky. 3 days before Christmas. My father was torn from our family.

> "I'm about to tell you the worst news you'll probably ever hear."
>
> —My mother, 12-22-11.

A piece of me was severed from my soul. Before that, I could have never imagined a Christmas without him. He was there, and that's how it was supposed to be. Nothing different. It smelled like pine, gingerbread, and all things merry. It was anything but. Broken, I collapsed. Gasping for breath I couldn't find. You would think I was too young to understand. I understood fully. I won't ever see him again. Ever. He's dead.

"It gets easier every day."

—Anyone ever who has lost a loved one.

It doesn't.

3 days before Christmas. Maybe it's just a coincidence. My brother. 6 months ago, he was born. My father. 6 years ago, he died.

2 years after that, my mom introduced my 2 siblings and me to another man. In 3 years, she would marry him. In 2 more, they would have a newborn son, my half-brother. He's 6 months now and it's almost Christmas. Hanging ornaments while blasting Christmas music from the kitchen. We eat cookies and drink hot chocolate topped with whipped cream and marshmallows. It's joyful, it's merry, it really does feel like a bright, happy Christmas.

Maybe this year . . . no. Sooner or later my mind will start to go dark again. Thinking about a thing that happened many years ago. 3 days before Christmas.

CHAPTER ONE

The landscape between my parents' home in Pennsylvania and the York Airport consists of rolling hills and two-lane roads. Normally, I would not have gone to the airport alone to pick up Brian—but it was Christmastime. Brian was Santa Claus, and the sleigh full of gifts was his airplane.

Santa's secrets needed to remain safe, so Melanie, Brooke, and Max stayed at home with my sister and mother, baking cookies and probably sprinkling red and green decorative sugar everywhere. My father, with prompting and prodding from my mother, was reluctantly shopping at Walmart for another mini-fridge to stock all the food and drinks our family would be happily consuming over the next few days. It was your typical holiday-week fun stuff. Excitement was building all around and it would all be made infinitely jollier with Brian's arrival.

When I tell you that the York County Airport is small, I mean it is *small*—smaller than many living rooms I've sat in. I had been speeding to get there, late because of a detour. I had been listening to music, and distinctly remember turning it down so I could concentrate better on the roads. I wouldn't be much good to anyone if I crashed on the way to pick up Brian.

A few miles from the airport, my cell phone rang. It was a

number I didn't recognize, from Washington, D.C.

I picked up, and the caller asked to speak to Brian Robertson.

"I'm sorry, this is his wife, Eileen, and I'm on my way to pick him up at the airport. Can I help you?"

The caller was from the National Transportation Safety Board (NTSB). Brian hadn't confirmed his landing. When I got to the airport, would I please ask him to call in as soon as possible? "Absolutely," I said, and then I apologized that he had forgotten.

The NTSB call made me nervous, but Brian had forgotten to call them before, and so I told myself not to overreact.

A couple of minutes later, I pulled into the parking lot and immediately noticed Brian's plane was not parked where it should have been. I jumped out of the car and rushed inside—leaving the car unlocked and my purse on the floor. I entered the small airport and asked about N48BS, confirming I was the pilot's wife. Someone said simply, "We believe that plane has gone down, Ma'am."

The first few moments are a blur, but the next thing I remember, I was outside in the cold, gripping a fence in the pitch-black country night.

"Think, Eileen, think!" What could I do? What should I do? I felt like I might faint. I tried to catch my breath.

I thought, Brian's plane was two nautical miles away, a distance I could cover in a sprint. But then my eyes seemed to stop blinking and my muscles tightened. I fell into a squat and willed myself to breathe.

I held on to that airport fence as if my life depended on it, and wanting to expel everything in my body. "Keep your shit together, Eileen," I said. "You don't know. You don't know anything yet."

A bright light was coming my way from the sky. It was the rescue helicopter that had been dispatched to search for Brian and, hopefully, save him. A rescue crew disembarked. If I said anything to them, I don't remember what it was.

While I was desperately trying not to assume the worst—because I knew that people *do* survive airplane crashes—one of the women from the helicopter crew put her arm around my shoulders and guided me inside.

I had never spent more than a few minutes inside that airport, but on December 22, 2011, I would spend almost two hours waiting for some kind of certainty.

Sitting with this information—the plane was down, and it was not possible to get to it, not immediately—what could I do? Absolutely nothing. I could do nothing but sit and wait. Time turned grotesquely in on itself, like a slug someone has poured salt on. I looked around at the airport and helicopter crew. They looked at me. I began to ask questions like, "Do you think he's alive? How damaged did the plane look? Did you see him at all? Do people survive crashes like that?"

There are a million classic movie scenes set at airports, where two people realize they cannot live without one another. Or they kiss one last time and go their separate ways. Or they—

What? What in the hell was happening? The airport crew was leaving!

Hey! Holidays or not, people—nobody leave. I need answers! Please.

A plane went down, they were thinking. Let's get the hell out of here!

Of course, I imagine my initial questions were . . . off target. One of the first responders, the woman who had led me, alone and unglued, back inside the York County Airport, never left my side. Talk about holding space and listening, this Search and Rescue crew member— probably wanting to get home to her family, too, to bake more cookies and wrap more presents—was my first angel. She did not have all the answers—I will never get all the answers. Nobody does.

But this angel, a woman whose name I don't remember, listened to me come at the "news"—N48BS crashed—from every angle.

"Hon," she would answer. "I don't know." Their helicopter had been asked to pull back. Fuel was on the ground surrounding Brian's plane, so they could not land safely and inspect the crash site. Ground crews had arrived on the scene and they would come and tell me more as soon as they could.

By this time, I had called my parents' home, where my other angels, my sister Mary Kay and my mother, were with Melanie, Brooke, and Max. Later, Mary Kay would tell me she knew, or could submit to the reality of the crash and Brian dying, before I could. She knew. But when I think of my sister and my mother holding down the fort, when time for them must have been unraveling too—I lose it. To this day, I lose it. I see them with Christmas tunes playing in the background and the terribly delicious smells of freshly baked reindeer-shaped Christmas cookies and the 12-foot Christmas tree, holding things together so that my kids could retain some semblance of normalcy for the last time ever. Mary Kay and my mother gave my children their last hour of a real childhood, when their innocence was still in place.

Although Mary Kay knew, my mother was probably doing what I was doing: holding on to the thinnest and shiniest tinsel of hope that Brian was somehow going to come out of this alive.

※

My mother and father raised us Catholic. And, though I haven't been a praying person since high school, I sent more prayers from the York County Airport out to the universe than the most fervent of worshippers. For ninety minutes, I prayed like a maniac to keep from wailing like a banshee. *Please, Lord Jesus, it's Christmas, for *%&#'s sake! Please, God, let him be alive. He can be in a wheelchair, lose a leg, be scarred from head to toe, but please, let him be okay.*

Adrenaline continued to surge through me but had no means of exit. There was no escape from my own convulsing inner organs. I wanted to vomit but didn't. If someone had told me I didn't blink for the entire two hours, I would have believed them.

Many people will tell you they physically sense when a loved one has passed. They can sense this from a distance even when the newly departed person should have been nowhere near their time for crossing over.

While I was still in limbo—after my father arrived but before the police and the coroner—a rush of lightness and energy passed through me.

No. No. No. I thought: *That better not have been you, Brian.*

Those plastic airport chairs. All of me felt swollen and at the same time deflated. I was as light as air. Lighter. Brian flooded my cells as he left. I would have floated away if not for my father.

My poor father. Jim. My resilient father. Jim McGuire. He had welcomed four children into the world: three of us remained. My sister Patricia—Tricia—died too soon. Tricia, too, died in December. On December 5, 1993, at around 1:00 p.m., my father picked up the phone and listened to the words that had crossed underground wires from Slippery Rock, Pennsylvania, to Crofton, Maryland—words that he could not ever have imagined he would have to hear. His youngest daughter had died in her sleep.

Life is supposed to go in order. We learn to walk, to use the potty, ride a bike; we go to grammar school, then to high school, then to college; we find a mate, marry, have babies; do meaningful work and help others; watch our children learn to walk, use the potty, ride a bike. Bask in their differences. Maybe one excels at a sport, one is great at school, another learns to fly a plane.

But children do not die before their parents. There is so much more expected and exceptional work to do.

Pleading, hoping, and worrying do not put life back in order, but boy, did I plead and hope and worry on that December evening. Damn, how I tried to squash and rework the worry.

I pleaded for someone, anyone—the angel from the helicopter, the man behind the counter at York County Airport, my father—to give me the one more detail that would help me make sense of this.

How long will it take to know if Brian is dead or alive? How long do I have to sit here? How much longer . . . ?

Had there not been a detour, would I have noticed, sooner, something amiss in the sky, in my cells?

I now know that Brian was already down by the time I had left my parents' house.

My father came through the door of the York County Airport with a distinct sense of urgency. He looked like a deer in the headlights. I don't know what I looked like to him, but whether he was hoping against all hope, as my mother was, or if he knew it in his bones as quickly as Mary Kay had, I am sure he could see in me the soul-leveling bewilderment he had experienced when he first received the news about Tricia.

My father, of course, was also breaking apart inside. He loved Brian and knew my love for him was deep and forever. The kids, his grandchildren—dear God, he would have prayed, help us rally around them. Despair closing in, he held his shit together for me. My entire family would do this, starting the minute we returned from the airport without Brian. But my father, as we sat with the unknown, was the father he had always been for me: fully present, warm, solid, capable.

I was still in rapid-fire questioning mode, and my father, like the helicopter angel, listened and answered: "I don't know, Eileen.

We'll find out. It will be all right. We'll have to wait and see." This was Jim McGuire in straight-up Dad mode. But, once the initial panicked rush to get to me receded, he also wore the look before crying. The contortion of the mouth, the tremble of the chin, every muscle of the face fighting against the wash of instant grief. My father held it together. For many long minutes, he did not let go.

And when we found out, for certain, together, that neither of us would see Brian alive again—that nobody would—we both lost it. The inner convulsions imploded. I was shaking. I reached for my phone as though I would be able to use it, but between tremors, I was literally (not literally) petrified. A stone. As much agony as I was in, I knew what was coming for Brian's parents, Dave, Donna, and sister, Julie—and I couldn't bear it. To this day, I can't explain my urge to avoid Brian's family for those first twenty-four hours, can't explain my ability to tell anybody but them that Brian had died.

Jim McGuire did not question his duty. The man who had raised me made the call. I listened, but only know he said, very calmly, something like: "Brian's plane went down, and he didn't make it."

Just as he'd held himself together for me, he had now pulled himself together for Brian's parents. My father knew what it was like to be on the receiving end of such news. And really, how else do you deliver this kind of message?

Life is not playing by the rules: You have lost a child.

My father's voice, so soothing—his telling, so matter-of-fact— made it hard to believe. *Brian didn't make it.* What an unreal statement. If it were true, how could anyone simply . . . say it?

＊

My father had always allowed me, his usually hyper-self-sufficient daughter, to present to him my most vulnerable side. With my father, I could be unapologetically myself. If I was in need of any help, I could be so without reservation. To this day, I'm working on the balance between pushing straight through a challenge without asking for help and going full-on HELP ME I CANNOT DO THIS ALONE!

But, nobody can grieve alone. All right, I've learned there are no rules in the grieving process, so I'll rephrase: Nobody should have to grieve alone. Without my family's support, who knows how or where I would be now?

The truth is, the grieving process is never-ending. People don't want to tell you that. They hope you'll consult some books, some experts, some therapists. Tricia, the sister I had shared a room with for over a decade of my life, died when I was twenty-three years old. I remember going to the library and checking out a stack of books on death, dying, mourning, grief, and closure. The books helped, but there is no closure. We move forward, but grief moves through time and space in surreal ways. I'll be cycling my heart out with my Peloton, and something—anything—will click and pierce my solar plexus. This is grief, and I am at peace with it. These moments are reminders not of what I've lost, but of what I have deeply loved.

CHAPTER TWO ·

I'm a lucky woman. The last words my husband and I exchanged before the Cessna Conquest he was flying went down two nautical miles from the landing strip were "I love you" and "I love you, too."

But that's not why I am okay now.

Brian's death took place more than seven years ago. And, although the passage of time does help, neither is this the sole reason I am okay.

Brian and I had three amazing children together, and in the hours, days, weeks, months, and years following his death, I could not fall apart. He had crashed with only one more turn to make. Crashing—for me, curling up in the fetal position under the covers and shouting to the sky, "This isn't fair!"—was not an option. I had to appear okay for Melanie, Brooke, and Max, who were eight, seven, and four years old at the time.

Whatever *okay* really means, I appeared to be holding it together as much as I could, for the kids and for Brian's spirit or memory or whatever you call the energy that never leaves your side. I admit, many times early on, I practiced FITYMI: "Fake it till you make it." I'm a believer in that mantra and have channeled it when I've needed to conquer things much less difficult than my husband's sudden and untimely death. That said, FITYMI doesn't fully explain why I am okay now—thriving, in fact—seven years later.

Thriving?

I know, right? But it's true. And one of the reasons why it's true is the certainty that Brian wouldn't want it any other way. He would kick my ass if I weren't kicking ass. I knew this man—son, brother, father, friend, entrepreneur, dreamer—like I knew my own skin.

Brian and I first met when we were members of a shared beach house on Martha's Vineyard during the summer of 1998. Originally, I'd wondered if I should join. Everyone who was invited seemed out of my league. They had graduated from either MIT or Harvard or held a ridiculously impressive job title, and I was sure none of them realized that inviting me had been a mistake. Sure, I could talk about denormalizing databases with the best of them in the late '90s, but insecurities affect us all. I had also recently broken up with my college boyfriend, Chris, whom I had been dating on and off for nine years, so parts of me felt uncentered.

The money was a factor too: This beach vacation would cost more than I'd ever spent on rest and relaxation in my life. But I needed to meet new people. Worst case scenario, I wouldn't make any friends and the money would be wasted. Best case scenario— isn't Martha's Vineyard where all the famous people hang out? I would meet and fall in love with George Clooney's doppelgänger. I told myself, "Just do it!"

The weekend started out with the usual beach activities— drinking Mudslides, swimming in the sea, barbecuing, and watching the sun set. My first impression of Brian was that he was nice and sweet but not my type. I'm tall, Brian was short—and, as shallow as it may sound, I'd always eliminated shorter men from my list of datable options. He was also only twenty-five, and I was turning twenty-eight that weekend. Surely he wasn't mature enough for me.

Mid-weekend, I went on a long run. I was training for the Honolulu Marathon. When I got back to the house, feeling invigorated and accomplished, I made a pitcher of Mudslides. (What better way to rehydrate?) Still partly dancing the tunes I'd put my miles into, I brought the elixir out to the backyard to share with whoever was hanging out. Brian was there, with his bags packed waiting for the taxi to come and take him to the ferry to go back to Boston.

I poured him a Mudslide and said, "Hey! Why don't you stay? It's my birthday!"

I remember walking up the stairs to take a shower and feeling surprised by hoping he would stay—why the hell did I care? He canceled the cab and said he would join us for a round of celebratory drinks. Why did he stay? It is all too easy to miss meeting the person who will radically alter our lives for the better. Clearly, the universe had something in store for us.

From that first weekend, our relationship was a whirlwind of conversation, travel, fun, and setting mutual goals and reaching new heights. We were energy exponentiated, and nobody doubted we were meant for each other.

"You two must be serious," a friend said. She noticed I had started to wear flats instead of wedges or heels. We laughed.

After fifteen months of dating, meeting each other's friends and families, and moving in together when we left Boston for Seattle, Brian asked me to marry him on Thanksgiving, at my parents' house. Though my mother and father were supportive of us as a couple, they weren't keen on the idea of our living together. When we stayed at their place, we slept in separate bedrooms. Exhausted from our cross-country red-eye flight, Brian and I napped—in our separate rooms—that first morning. I woke up before he did and went downstairs to greet my family. I asked Patrick, my three-year-old nephew, if he wanted to wake up Brian.

Upstairs, Brian told Patrick to take me to my room because there was a present on my pillow. "I'll meet you both there," Brian said.

Patrick could hardly contain his excitement—he snatched my hand and dragged me up to my room. I immediately saw the box. It was a ring box. What was happening? I alternated between looking at Patrick and looking at Brian and then told Patrick to go downstairs and tell everyone Brian and I would be right down.

"Are you sure?" was all I could say. This was not how I had pictured the big romantic moment exactly.

"Yes, I'm sure. Will you marry me?"

"Yes, of course!"

At our wedding, my friend Joe sang "We Live on Borrowed Time" during the prelude at the church.

※

My late husband and I were deeply connected. And so I know Brian doesn't mind that I now am remarried and have had another baby (at age forty-six!), because—yes, wait for it—Brian is the one who actually set us up. Before Mike Hamra, my now husband, and I ever had our first date, both he and I had crazy vivid dreams where Brian appeared and gave us permission and direction to go for it. Now, I realize not everyone has a loved one die and then stick around to support them, so I asked Mike, "Are you okay with this? You know, there is an 'extra person' in this relationship . . ."

I was pretty sure the recognition of the reality that, beyond what we could have chalked up as oddly lucid and similar dreams, would have him running for the door, but Mike did not run. He stuck around. Clearly, he was fine with all of it.

And clearly, I've been blessed by the love of two self-assured and generous men.

But stop me. I'm going way too fast. In the past seven years and, really, in the past couple of decades since my sister died, I've been lucky. Call me woowoo, that's fine—*I am semi-woowoo*—but my deceased loved ones have my back. They play jokes on me. There have been dreams and daydreamy visits. There have been ridiculous coincidences—signs. I don't doubt that Brian, a man who died between two silver wings, and Tricia, a young woman whose heart fluttered off-beat, watch over me like angels—funny, smart, talented, driven, and dedicated angels. This, too, is part of the reason I am okay; I am thriving.

For me to be able to speak now of gratitude and joy feels so different from when I experienced, within months of Brian's passing, the first pangs of truth in knowing that I would survive and would even be happy again. Someone once accused me of "speed grieving."

But another person, my amazing father, one day responded to my barely whispered question, "Is it okay that I'm okay, Dad? I don't think I should feel okay right now. Maybe I'm in denial?"—"Eileen, there are no *shoulds*. There is no 'right' way to grieve. When you're sad, be sad. When you're okay, be okay. Don't try being something you're not."

Why I am okay and able to say I am lucky, when others can't or won't, is in some ways a mystery to me. But if some force or chance or fate taking away my sister when she was twenty and Brian when he was thirty-eight isn't a mystery, then I don't know what is. For all the dreaming and planning and organizing we do, for all the promise each single life holds from womb to whenever, death often comes at the wrong time and rips open the fabric of our being.

*

I am lucky, but I'm not clueless. I understand that the notion of owning one's own airplane remains merely a notion for most people—a marker of success, a status symbol. Rock stars own planes. (You know I'm going to say it: Brian was a rock star, even though he could only sing well in the shower.)

Since Brian was a boy, he'd had a thing for planes. I was never sure he would get one, but then we bought land in Mexico, and many of our neighbors were pilots. They were all older—Brian at the time wasn't yet thirty—but the thought of bringing one more fan of flying under their wings thrilled them. They gave him stacks of piloting magazines.

In 2002, Brian went back to business school in Boston. "Ah," he decided. "This is a good time to take pilot lessons!" And that was that.

After I gave birth to our first child, Melanie, we moved to Palo Alto for Brian's summer internship. Soon enough, the three of us were in the air, in a Cessna four-seater. We took the opportunity of this newfound freedom to zip down to Carmel and Monterey, to walk on the beach and visit the aquarium. I was never too afraid on these family flights; I trusted Brian. He went all in, no matter what he did, and flying was no different. He was a skilled pilot from the start.

Some days, we'd take off with no true destination—we'd putter around in the sky. Flying in an aircraft no bigger than a Volkswagen Beetle at 10,000 feet above the San Francisco Valley, with Melanie strapped to my chest in a Baby Bjorn, I did wonder who I was in the grand scale of things. Flight offers escape and perspective. Sometimes back then, I would marvel at how, most of the time, most of us go about our business drifting completely detached from the preciousness of life.

And then Brian and I would land and do whatever had to be done. We'd meet our obligations.

After we moved back to Boston for his second year at Harvard

Business School, Brian decided to go *even more all in* than all in: He logged miles toward his commercial license and then did acrobatic training. Yes, my stomach flipped a little at the thought of him spinning around up there in circles, doing corkscrews or infinity rings or whatever pilots call them. But he read voraciously and constantly about flying. He wanted to be prepared for the "what if." The guy I married was normally a risk taker, and I loved that about him; but with flying, he was super by-the-book. He made checklists and followed protocol.

Before and after takeoff and landing, without fail, we followed a ten-minute no-talking rule. The majority of airplane accidents take place during these two critical phases of flying, and Brian gave all his focus to keeping his precious cargo safe. The three kids, as young as they were, learned to zip their lips for this ritual. Sometimes when our family flies together now, on a commercial plane, I close my eyes and think what magic it would be if every passenger observed this silence.

Slowly, in the name of practicality, Brian bought bigger and bigger planes. The bigger the plane, the faster you go, the less often you have to make a landing to refuel, and the more time you can save. You can get bigger planes only when you have enough flying hours. You've got to log time in the plane you want to fly, flying with a copilot for hours, and so on. I didn't pay much attention to the number of hours Brian was putting in up there, but I knew that our main reason for owning a plane was to make life easier.

My parents lived in Pennsylvania, not far from the York County

Airport. Brian's parents lived in Bancroft, Ontario, Canada. Brian had N48BS modified so we could make cross-country trips to visit our families frequently, without stopping.

✳

"There was a time when I believed that life held guarantees. There was a time when I was sure my future was secure."

—David Friedman

The song our friend Joe sang at our wedding was the same song he would sing at two of the memorial services held for Brian: "We Live on Borrowed Time." Talk about full circle.

Do some people have a sense of how much or how little time they have? Brian was not only a mover and a shaker in his professional life—he sold one of his companies to Amazon, he became an up-and-coming maverick in the solar industry—but he was a mover and shaker at home as well. In our household, there was no such thing as a chill, lazy weekend. No way, no how! Before our first child was born, our days were filled with activity. I had planned most of our wedding, but our honeymoon was Project Brian. On our eight-day vacation in Mexico we played golf four times, rented ATVs, jet-skied, snorkeled, rode horses, went on a desert hike, had dinner reservations every night, and indulged in several spa treatments. In between all of this, Brian read eight novels, *and* we put in an offer to buy property.

Absolutely nothing irritated Brian more than wasting time. Did he know his time was limited?

My sister, Tricia, spent the bulk of her time in the swimming pool, doing what she loved. She was a world-class water polo player. Have you ever played water polo? Water polo was an extreme sport before the concept of extreme sports existed! If Tricia wasn't in the pool, she was hanging with her many friends, always looking for adventure.

If Brian or my sister were the type to get tattoos, "I'll sleep when I'm dead" would have been etched onto every cell in their bodies—in luminescent ink. Google *luminescent*. Wikipedia will tell you that, "The dials, hands, scales, and signs of aviation and navigational instruments and markings are often coated with luminescent materials in a process known as 'luminising.'" Light inside the cockpit can literally show a pilot the way home to his loved ones.

I loved Brian and Tricia and their inner light, their energy.

Physicists tell us energy cannot be destroyed. So, after someone dies, where does their energy go? Does it pass through us on its way to somewhere else? Does it linger, move like waves, find us again years down the road to shoot through us so viscerally we stop in the middle of spin class and look in the mirror, over our shoulder?

After someone dies suddenly, in an attempt to hold on to and maintain the live connection you shared, that back-and-forth force that sustained you both, you do look back—you pore over every detail, clue, hint, message, silence, act. Was there something I missed? Was I paying attention? Did they know this was coming—have a hunch? Was there static on their radar: "Pssst. Hey you. Be sure you've got all loose ends tied up. Make it a point to hug your loved ones."

After someone dies, we save their texts, even the most mundane ones. We keep the voice messages.

Words—we hang on to them. Voices—they are an intricate and impactful result of breathing, of being alive. If the tech geniuses ever invent a way to capture the smell of the people we have loved, they'll make billions.

A few hours after Brian dropped me and the kids off at the Orange County California Airport to fly east for Christmas—just one week before he died—Brian texted me: *I feel really sad you aren't here with me right now.* It was an uncharacteristic message. This was a man who sang in the shower before his first cup of coffee. What was that sadness? Our usual texts and voicemails are easy to imagine: an entrepreneurial couple with three young children and a rescued Chihuahua mutt tap out logistics and the occasional love note. Most of our daily cell phone exchanges were ordinary: "Can you think of anything else we need while I'm at the store?" and "What's your ETA?"

I went over Brian's "I feel really sad" text countless times. We had shared such an amazing and intimate night twenty-four hours before he wrote that to me, one hundred and sixty-eight hours before he would leave countless people so bereft. So shocked. So numbed and confused.

When we accidentally delete a text as silly as, "Miss you, honey

"Wink wink?" it can throw us into a tailspin.

Tailspin.

Brian came down.

The right engine failed. He was two nautical miles from landing and just 1,100 feet in the air when it happened. While chaos in the cockpit was building, crash reports showed that he remained calm. The Brian I knew was absolutely sure he would regain control of his airplane, until he didn't. If anything could have been done, he would have done it.

Brian's ETA was 5:32 p.m., December 22, 2011. I had been following his plane on flighttracker.com: It told me he was 330 nautical miles out, and then 110 nautical miles, and then two. Stuck on two. At first, I thought, "That's odd." I refreshed the screen multiple times: *2 nm, 2 nm, 2 nm.* I called Brian to confirm he was on the ground, but his phone went to voicemail. A little odd, but still, at this point, I was not yet overly concerned: I knew he would be busy doing the post-flight checklist. Brian Robertson was a meticulous flyer. And besides, I was running late, and he'd be upset if I made him wait too long. It had been a long week apart, and I wanted to kiss him the way I was planning to kiss him.

Had Brian's plane failed at any other time, higher in the sky or farther from landing, he probably would have made it. Had he made his final turn, he could probably have glided in. But we live on borrowed time: "Life had other plans."

Life is supposed to roll forward; but most of us, no matter how consciously we try to appreciate the present moment and not take anything for granted, drop the ball from time to time. I look back on the things that used to pull my irrational "Scary Mommy" reaction string, and I sigh and smile and sometimes laugh. What a huge wake-up call becoming a single parent overnight is. And still, all these years later, I have to mindfully practice saving space for my children—I still have to catch myself. Scary Mommy is always ready to be invoked if I forget for one moment what I used to catch glimpses of, up above in that plane. We don't have much time together here.

CHAPTER THREE

Prior to age twenty-three—the age I was when my little sister Tricia died—I had flown on an airplane just twice. In middle school, I was a pretty good swimmer, and our team was going to fly from Washington, D.C., to Orlando, Florida, to compete. On the way to the airport, my mother had to pull the car over to the side of the road so I could throw up. The combination of nervousness and excitement at this first taste of adventure caused me to puke again on the plane.

My stomach fared better a decade later, on my second flight ever, though I still recall my mind being blown away by the fact that I could be in one place one minute, and another place so entirely different a few hours later.

At twenty-two, I was on the board of the local Washington, D.C., chapter of the Holiday Project, a nonprofit organization my parents had introduced my brother and sisters and me to after we stopped believing in Santa Claus. The Holiday Project collects gifts such as hand lotion and blankets and delivers them to people in prisons, nursing homes, and hospitals. Feeling like something of a bigwig, or at least confident that I was a leader coming into my own, I was thrilled to be invited to a conference in Arizona. I had never traveled farther west than West Virginia.

I can distinctly recall being on that flight to Phoenix, wide awake, l was looking out the window as the pilot steered us up and into the clouds. I remember crying—happy-crying. Why was I so emotional? It's hard to say for sure, but part of it was the overwhelming awareness of the newness of everything. My father has always said, "The extraordinary soon becomes the ordinary." But for me, that trip was anything but ordinary, and it still serves to remind me of the value of bringing a beginner's mind to some of the tasks, activities, and capabilities we take for granted.

The flight to Phoenix signified a shift. Over broad expanses of farmland, divided into circles and squares of varying greens and browns, over highways and roadways that spread like human veins and arteries, all linked in one self-contained, complex, and usually super-efficient life-sustaining system, the airplane I was flying in floated through the sky like a great whale. *Holy crap,* I thought. *I'm an adult, and this is a big wide world, and I'm cruising at 30,000 feet over the arc of it.* In those cities below, under the shadows of glinting skyscrapers, hundreds of thousands of people were living their completely unique lives, sleeping and waking and eating and birthing and dying in a miraculously orchestrated and impossibly unending flow.

I'm not saying I loved flying as much as Brian did, or that I see what he saw up there, or that I still experience mind-blowing awe whenever I fly, but most of us have flashes of flights we have taken eternally etched into our consciousness. Clouds will always seem to me like giant puffy pillows you could sumptuously fall into. There is wonder in flight. Wonder in discovery. Wonder in leaving and, we hope, in returning home.

Approaching the edge of the Sonoran Desert that surrounds Phoenix, I could see nothing but heat rising in wiggly blinding waves from a flat sand horizon, but I felt the vastness of the so much more that was out there. Call me young, call me an East Coast fool, but at twenty-two I was so eager to be out in this *something more*—this something so different the pilot could have told me we had landed on Mars and I would have believed him—that I decided to climb Camelback Mountain in July. (You know you're volunteering for a nonprofit when they hold their annual conference in Arizona in mid-summer—right?) But even back then, I knew to be grateful—for the opportunity with the Holiday Project, for my newfound appreciation of clouds, for the desert air at 5 a.m., and for my legs, which carried me straight to the top of that dry orange mountain.

I was only twenty-two on that trip, but grateful for being alive.

Camelback Mountain is also known as Sacred Mountain, for the numerous Native American holy artifacts archaeologists have unearthed there. One of the mountain's most unusual features is a red sandstone formation named "The Praying Monk." Of course, rock climbers scramble all over it now, but back then the Monk was undisturbed. Back then, although I was deeply involved with an organization that served others, I was not active in the church and didn't pray much. But the day I traversed the humps of Camelback Mountain, my spirit shifted gears; that day, I knew I would always need to press beyond the familiar to feel free.

On that blazing July day, there wasn't a cloud in the sky. The blue of it was nothing like the blue I knew in Maryland or anywhere

I had ever been. It is known that high noon in most places is the worst time to take photographs. In Phoenix and in the Salt River Valley, the midday light is so bright everything seems to freeze. Colors fade. Even the red-hued Praying Monk is drained of his essence. At high noon, shadows cease to exist. You see in 2-D.

You lose a dimension.

In hot southwestern places, you understand the logic behind the siesta, the stilling of your breath, the slowing of your heart rate. The hike was hard. Focused on taking one step at a time and breathing with intent, I drew upon my deepest strength—and kept going. As I recall it now, the climb to the top of Camelback Mountain felt like a prayer.

*

Nuns, the Daughters of Charity specifically, were my teachers. From first through twelfth grade, I attended Catholic school and was taught how to live a moral life following the Ten Commandments. In the mid-1970s, our public school district was desegregated, and that early exposure to life outside the suburbs shaped me. On the long bus ride to school, I would see families standing with all their earthly possessions on the side of the road, being evicted from their homes. At the end of the day, around the dinner table, my family discussed matters beyond "How was school?" We figured out ways to practice what we were learning, and we learned from what we were witnessing. We fed the homeless and regularly practiced acts of charity. I was taught to be nonjudgmental.

My father, who worked as a NASA engineer his entire life, was educated by the open-minded Jesuits. My mother, who stayed at home to raise us, has a faith so strong, she could pray anyone out of hell.

Growing up, I believed the notion that God was the Father in the sky who loved me, protected me, and would ultimately judge whether I was a good or bad girl—worthy of eternal heaven or hell. But as a young woman, I began questioning this patriarchal vision of who and what guides us.

Moving through my own journey, experiencing love and loss, birth and death, the old notions of my spirituality seemed limiting. I've come to adapt what you could call a "buffet-style" spirituality—a little Catholic, a little Hindu, a little California modern-day woo-woo. As we experience life, I believe that we continually lose our naïveté, our innocence. First, we are tossed from the security of the womb. Growing up, we get "dropped" and hurt. We learn to survive small losses and big ones, and in the process we often lose sight of our safe shores. We become more detached from the love we were all born of—the original love, the universal. Losing our innocence is a forgetting of where we came from.

Before I traveled west that first time, I had grown up in a relatively safe bubble and was naïve about the world at large, with all of its wonders and dangers, its lightness and darkness. Now, when I find myself settling into any kind of bubble, I don't dwell on the fact that they all eventually burst, but I do believe that moments when the iridescent film goes "POP!" are actually opportunities to wake up and see more vividly.

Before I traveled west the first time, my sister Patricia was alive, a star water polo goalie—a protector. The role was familiar to her and might have started in kindergarten, when she was already a head taller than most of her classmates, boys included. But regardless of her stature, her friends always felt safe and happy when they were with her.

Tricia and I were the water babies of the McGuire clan. I swam competitively from ages five to eighteen. Tricia also started swimming at five. She was better than I, and beat all my records, and when she played her first water polo game at age eleven, she got hooked. By the time she was thirteen, she was practicing with the Naval Academy's Junior Team in Annapolis. Quickly discovering how talented she was, her coaches had her practice with the Academy's college team. Tricia McGuire was a teenaged girl in the pool with a bunch of young college men, and she held her own.

My little sister earned a scholarship to Pennsylvania's Slippery Rock team, and when I say *earned*, I mean it: as goalie, she suffered broken fingers and concussions. The Slippery Rock women's water polo team, for the record, was noted in an online article in the "Lest We Forget: The Pioneers of Women's Water Polo" series as, historically, being "THE team on the east coast . . . , the most organized and most competitive."

In 1992, Tricia earned her spot on the Senior National Women's team, and began to travel the world representing the United States at the World Cup and other tournaments.

Women's water polo became an Olympic sport in 2000. Tricia died in 1993. At her induction into the Water Polo Hall of Fame in Annapolis, in 2017, the U.S. Senior National Coach said that, had the (women's) sport made the Olympic roster earlier, and had she lived longer, Tricia would have been the goalie for the first women's U.S. Olympic team. Standing beside the pool where she had practiced thirty years prior, nobody doubted it. All her coaches and teammates talked about her incredible work ethic in the pool. She would run drills until she was so exhausted she risked drowning.

Technically, my sister wasn't supposed to overdo it in sports. Tricia was the only kid in the family who wore glasses, she sleep-walked, she snored so loudly she had to have her adenoids removed, and she had knee and back surgery before age eighteen. At age twelve, after a coach said he thought Tricia was having panic attacks in the pool, my parents took her to the doctor. Naturally, she would be the one to be diagnosed with a heart condition.

Wolff-Parkinson-White Syndrome, in basic terms, occurs in people born with an extra electrical pathway in their heart. When a stimulus pumps through this circuit that should not be there, the heart races at a dangerous pace, causing lightheadedness and short-ness of breath. In worst case scenarios, it can cause a heart attack.

In junior high, my sister was put on the anti-arrhythmic drug Tambocor to regulate her heartbeat, and, though it was risky for her to engage in a sport as insanely demanding as water polo, what were my parents supposed to do? Deny their athletically gifted child the primary outlet for her gift? What would you or I do, as a parent? My children are athletically daring, and I give them freedom even when it terrifies me, maybe because I know not only how short childhood is but how short adulthood can be too.

The last time I saw my sister, two weeks before she died, she was not herself. Tricia stood 5'10" and weighed in at a lean and in-the-water-mean 135 pounds. You should have seen her wingspan. At Thanksgiving, she looked pale, she was lethargic. Everyone in the family knew the past year had taken its toll on her. While she was kicking ass in the pool, pieces of her body, mind, and spirit were struggling to keep afloat.

The previous December, her good friend had hanged herself. Tricia was haunted by her suicide, and by the belief that she should have known something was horribly wrong, that she should have been able to protect her. Then, the following July, right after I returned from Arizona, Tricia underwent surgery to burn away the unwanted extra electrical pathway in her heart.

My sister was young and strong; she was a great candidate for surgery. As it turned out, though, of all the places those extra pathways to the heart can be, Tricia's was in the most dangerous location. The coronary specialist team at Johns Hopkins wondered if a better medical team might exist out there for her. Their struggle to come up with the right plan added to Tricia's stress, but she remained hopeful about the surgery and the prospect of being meds-free afterward.

Ultimately, when the Johns Hopkins team opened my sister's heart, they found more than one excess pathway around it. They could not remove them all. One of the best coronary teams in the country had cut into the very core of her, and, though they made her heart better, they broke it, too. Her heart could not be fixed; she would still need to take medication. My sister fell further into depression and added Prozac to her medications.

On December 4, Tricia complained of feeling ill, and her friends went with her to the hospital in Slippery Rock. The doctors there knew her well because of her multiple water polo injuries and her heart condition. They ran an EKG; all was normal. No bloodwork was done. Had the doctor taken that one extra step, he might have noticed that the Prozac Tricia was taking was preventing her heart medicine from metabolizing properly. The very medicine she was taking to save her life had been poisoning her for the last four months.

CHAPTER FOUR

There is little, if any, value in hindsight. I know this, but I know too that, as much as we're supposed to be focusing on the present and enjoying the moment and *namaste namaste namaste*, moving through grief does require going back to the tough spots at times. On this long curving path of grief, we sometimes need to retrace our journey. We revisit the forks in the road, and let in the anger, the anguish, and the what-the-fuck hopelessness all over again.

In 2011, it was my father who called Brian's parents to deliver the news that is never deliverable. My father understood how it felt to be on the receiving end of such a phone call. Eighteen years prior, he had been home alone when the Slippery Rock campus staff contacted him. He had just sat down to watch the Redskins game.

Tricia's college roommates were concerned that she was sleeping in too late that day and went to her room to wake her. Sometime around noon on December 5, 1993, everyone in Tricia's circle—roommates, teammates, coaches, professors, friends, and family—lost a dimension. Now, instead of four children, my parents had three. Their baby girl was gone. The world would lose color, energy, spirit.

While he was taking their words in—not wanting to believe them and thinking *no no no no no*—my sister Mary Kay beeped through via call waiting.

My heart drops when I think of my father gripping the phone, with the football announcers droning on in the background and nobody there to steady his body when it felt like crumbling, no angel or stranger with him to answer the dozens of questions racing through his brain. I can see his mouth quivering as he repeats to Mary Kay the words that had just passed his ear and shot to his heart. I can feel the blood in his veins rushing up his neck, constricting his throat, flushing his cheeks and ears, setting his flesh on fire while simultaneously turning it cold. His daughter, with every muscle so strong but one, her heart, was dead. He told Mary Kay this. And then, in a stunned and robotic state, he hung up and called my brother, and then left a message for me with my roommate.

My sister, my brother, and my brother's wife rushed over and were at my parents' home before my mother returned from shopping. They watched my father go out to the garage when they heard it open. My mother's screaming and wailing lasted for what seemed like forever. Everyone went to the garage and gathered together to hold her—to do what? To let it sink in that her child had died.

Sink, this kind of news does.

December 5, 1993, my family would stop breathing, on and off, for what felt like hours, days, and weeks at a time.

✳

When the policeman and the coroner told me that Brian had not survived his plane crash, I wouldn't believe them. *No. No. There must have been a mistake.* They told me to sit down. Why? To control me? Had they been here before? Were they preparing for some mad, some primal outburst of grief and despair? Was it to protect me? To protect them? Maybe the first split seconds of grief—the pre-grief ripping apart of the heart from its known universe—were the worst moments to which anyone could ever bear witness.

Who knows why our immediate reaction to loss is the urge to tear our skin apart or fall flat to the earth shouting *why?*

What I do know is that I am intimate with the gaping hole of hell, and, contrary to popular belief, hell is all darkness. There is no fire. There is no light.

Once upon a time, when I was more innocent and naïve, I flew to Phoenix and discovered that light could completely devour shadow. In the Valley of the Sun, on Camelback Mountain, I walked, prayed, and happy-cried under the gaze of the Standing Monk. I wouldn't have been thinking then about the imagery and myth of the phoenix, a yellow and orange firebird that rises out of the char and ashes to be born again, and again, and again. I was probably thinking about drinking some water and eating a granola bar. But years later I have the capacity, the distance, and the new life experiences to make the connections between these terribly different moments: to fly, to cry at high altitude, to experience freedom, to lose a dimension.

I can now wonder too: If an engineer, a doctor, a pharmacist, some inspector somewhere had noticed this or that and said something, would my sister and Brian still be alive? It is fruitless to argue with reality; I know this. But the "ifs" can be tempting.

The *ifs* can be endless.

If can mean absolutely nothing.

If can uncover secrets and leave them forever unanswerable.

If can walk the grateful and gut-wrenching line.

What *if* Brian and I hadn't been in one of our more loving phases of marriage—if we hadn't been exchanging "I miss yous" and "I love yous," and had instead been arguing, via text, about some meaningless or meaningful thing?

If can introduce wishes: if only our favorite human beings could still be with us.

If Tricia had become an aunt.

If only I knew where the dead go.

I can't know for sure where those I've lost are, but I've learned to be okay with believing the dead—my dead, anyway—are in some way with me. There are times when they make me laugh in signs they randomly toss my way, and in memories.

The weight of profound loss takes its time before it can possibly transform into anything beyond heartbreaking. But eventually the *no*s turn toward *yes*es, and then land in a soft and accepting *okay*.

I've got my angels, and I've got my work cut out for me. We all do, really. I learned a lot about light and darkness in my early twenties. I learned that you never know how loved you are until tragedy strikes. I learned that community steps in and saves you from drowning, but that, when the surge of food and comforting arms and goodwill recedes, you still have to do the work of the living.

When I meet people now who are where I was right after my sister died and right after Brian died, I remember my first angel at the airport in Pennsylvania. The stranger who sat with me, allowing me to question away. To this day, I wonder what I would have done without her.

When I meet people who are grieving or "pre-grieving," I remember all the unanswerable questions, the confusion about the undeliverable news that they have received, and I try my best to calm my breathing, slow my heartbeat. I try my best to be that angel in some small way, to meet them where they are and to stand alongside them for as long as it takes.

✳

During a total eclipse of the sun, we finally see the corona. Weird shadows play on the ground. Birds stop singing and bats fly. The light takes on a quality of something between "the calm before the storm" and "apocalyptic." The temperature, no matter where we are, chills. People stop what they're doing—we stop time and gather—to watch and to feel this together. So, what if it is true that the only way to appreciate light and warmth, joy and the sun that sustains us, is to set it all against darkness, hell, tears, and the abyss of loss? What if we are all phoenixes, each of us capable of flying after a crash?

Brian's body is gone, Tricia's too, but they live on through the arteries, veins, networks, waves, pathways, circles, and cycles of this universe. They live on through the promises we made to them and follow through on. They live on through the sheer simple promise of who they were and who they would have become.

I am okay sitting with the mystery of why the good ones are taken, because I know there is no satisfying answer to that question. And, honestly, inviting the mystery in takes me closer to the source—whether we call that source God, Allah, a higher power, or the place where the living and the dead exchange energy. I am as practical as can be, but I freaking dance with mystery in my kitchen. I know shitty things happen to good people and that, while you're in the shit, it can be impossible to see a way out. It's so hard to simply continue to get out of bed, to move, to explore, to climb some sacred mountain when all we want to do some days is hide and cry and kick and scream. It feels blasphemous, or disrespectful, or selfish and insane to think that, beyond the despair, we might one day love more than we ever thought possible.

Most of the time, life does not feel like a fairy tale. We allow the extraordinary to become ordinary to the extent that some days it is impossible to recognize what we do have. But our angels are everywhere, and they show up when we need them. On a given day, all we need to hear from them is what Dory, the surgeonfish, said to Nemo, the clownfish: "Just keep swimming." Another day, when we can't move our arms and kick our legs at the same time, those angels hold us and keep us afloat.

One day, we are called to be the godmother, the angel, the ally that sits with the stranger in the small airport, or drops everything to drive hours to do nothing but *be there*.

✳

Growing up in an Irish Catholic church-going family, I learned there was power in prayer, and boy, did I pray at the York County Airport: *Please, God, change this. Fix this. I'll do anything. Please, God, just let Brian be alive.*

Mine was a desperate prayer that night in December, and, though I did not get what I asked for, I do believe my prayer was answered. I received everything I needed at that time. My family and I are incredibly fortunate to have communities that have showed up for us and shown us abundant love. Life without family, friends, and love is undoable, unimaginable to me. We come from love, I believe. Love is the source. As we grow, we experience one loss of innocence, and then another, and another, and so on. But as long as we have guides—people and spirits supporting us—these losses can be portals into still more love.

We carry love in our hearts all along, hopefully, but as we come into adulthood, daily tasks and necessities pull at us. With our hands and bodies and minds, we get stuff done. With our eyes and ears, we focus and believe in only what we see and hear. We move from Point A to Point B on the veins and arteries—the roadways, flightpaths, and sea lanes—that connect us. We pack and unpack our luggage. We are soccer and ballet moms, spending too much time packing and unpacking our children from our mom taxis.

And this is how, before we know it, the mundane takes over the sacred. The extraordinary becomes ordinary.

I wouldn't trade my life for anyone's, and not because my life is perfect. It sometimes is, and it sometimes isn't. Hell is a split second away from ensnaring any of us, always. Except at high noon, light casts shadows. This is not some poetic bullshit: Shadows are part us, part earth and sky, and part what we have built here. We need to be comfortable standing in them, letting them pass overhead, letting them chase and chill us. As long as we can promise ourselves to take the time every now and then—in the best of times and in the worst of times—to close our eyes and remember who we were before any loss, we will be okay. We will heal and we will reconnect with love, the source, our own core essence.

CHAPTER FIVE

The plan for Christmas 2011 was typical: *One clan gathers at one home one day, and, the next day, half that crew hops in a car or a plane to join another clan elsewhere.* On December 22, the festive, jolly, eager holiday spirit was in full swing at my parents' home. When I left to pick up Santa Claus at the airport that evening, my sister Mary Kay and my mom were keeping the kids busy rolling out dough and cutting cookies. The kitchen was warm and sugary. Soup was cooking in the crockpot. Mom had the Christmas music playing, probably Bing Crosby and Nat King Cole crooning "Winter Wonderland" and "Silent Night." Dad was fearlessly battling last-minute crowds, picking up the mini fridge. My brother and his family would arrive the next day.

The tree was decorated and lit, Max's section probably a little too crowded with ornaments and tinsel. The evening was crisp. There was no snow on the ground, but there was always the promise of a white Christmas in South Central Pennsylvania. Driving to the airport, taking that detour, I passed house after house neatly outlined in red, green, and white lights. Electric reindeer grazed in sprawling country yards among blinking snowmen and dancing elves.

Each of us was filled with anticipation. We would watch *A Charlie Brown Christmas* on TV; we would stuff ourselves with ham, mashed potatoes, pie, and cookies; we would read Christmas books to the kids and take luxurious mid-afternoon naps. Even Brian would take a short snooze in the La-Z-Boy. The kids would play with their cousins; they'd stay awake as late as possible to hear Santa's sleigh bells and Rudolph's landing on the roof. In the morning they would wake before the crack of dawn and rip into wrapping paper under the tree.

I had mistletoe on my mind.

Brian would land and button things up with the plane, and we would spend what little alone time we had catching up before the madness.

But on that cold December night in the Pennsylvania countryside the whir of helicopter blades cut straight and hard through the promise of Christmas.

I arrived at the airport in a bit of a rush, after having received the call from the NTSB and pulling up to see no sign of N48BS. I parked my car and ran into the airport to find out where he was.

I would enter the airport and ask one of the two or three people working there, "Can you please tell me the status of November Four Eight Bravo Sierra?" I would be asked who I was: "I'm Eileen Robertson, the pilot's wife." I would be told, "Hold on," and would consider this holding hopeful: *If there were a problem, they would have told me.*

And then came the line: "I'm sorry, ma'am, but we believe that plane has gone down."

Some words, you never imagine coming together in your head: *Please let my husband be alive.*

"Too much fuel spillage to investigate immediately," my airport angel said.

I'll do anything, God—whoever—whatever—if you just bring Brian through that door.

✳

In the movie *Sliding Doors*, Gwyneth Paltrow's life course is changed—for better and for worse—in the split second when she misses boarding her usual subway train. The movie runs along two parallel story lines, and essentially pivots on one big "if." Surely, a life without Brian was not meant to be my alternate track, my big "if," my reality.

A single, random, seemingly small act, a split in the road, a tear in the fabric of what we call routine, or forever, can alter the rest of our days. The wife who awaits her husband, the kids who await their father, the in-laws awaiting the pilot with a plane full of presents—they would all crash when the news of the downed plane hit them. Some will "just know" the person so many love is gone before official confirmation: My sister Mary Kay understood before I did that her final hour with my children at our parents' house was in many ways their last hour of innocence.

Can I say it was their last hour of being whole? I don't know, because I like to believe that with love we eventually patch back up or fill back in the cracks that fracture our universe. But thinking of Melanie, Brooke, and Max baking, playing, and eating soup in those hours before I returned from the airport with my father that night, still puts a lump in my throat. Melanie, Brooke, and Max would never see their daddy alive again.

Under the best of circumstances, adults protect, support, and guide children. Husbands and wives protect, support, and guide each other. Long before the crash, before we had kids, Brian had hired an estate planner. As a businessman with a private plane, he was cautious.

But weeks before the crash, I had woken up to an email from Brian that began, "In case of my early demise" and included all the directions I would need in case something happened to him.

"WTF, dude?" I'd said to that.

WTF was right. When the police officer and coroner told me that Brian had not survived the crash, I admit, I immediately thought: *We have life insurance. The kids and I will be fine. Financially, we will be okay.*

In the split second of receiving the news of his death, though, I became a single mother. I know now—even with sound finances and support—parenting is the toughest full-time job on the planet, and nobody should have to go at it alone. My friends who "do" single parenthood have my full respect and support until my dying day. We do what we have to do, we adapt, we function, we even thrive, but had Brian not provided for us the way he did, and had we not been immediately surrounded and buffered by friends and family— I don't know if I'd be saying so often, "I'm a lucky woman." I've always adhered to a silver lining, pull-yourself-up-by-your-bootstraps mentality, but, when parenting alone, there are days you can't find your damn boots to put them on.

And the kids—Christmas week into the new year, February into that first Father's Day without their dad—how in the hell were they going to make it? Where would we go from there?

One of the lessons, I think, Brian's death presented us with is that we now know that, despite the best of plans, intentions, and dreams, we inevitably encounter detours. We may be forced far out of our way into strange and unfamiliar territory. This doesn't mean after Brian's death I single-parented with constant heaviness and gloom. It's not that we don't trust the universe or that we live in constant fear of losing one another, but I think the kids and I—even Max, who had no idea at first what hit him—understand the precious value of good days.

We survived our worst day ever: I walked through my parents' front door that starlit December night to shouts of "Daddy! Daddy! Daddy!"

But the only Daddy there was mine.

Immediately, I sat the children down on my parents' maroon-flowered couch. It is the job of the adult to put into words . . . to first find the words . . . to somehow speak the terrible truth. I started.

I said, "I have some really bad news."

"Oh what, Daddy couldn't come?"

Children can't fathom the most horrible possibilities when, so far, their lives have consisted of nothing but: *Go for it, anything is possible, try, let's see!*

"He had to cancel?"

Nothing in their voices indicated they had a clue of what was coming next.

If you don't say the words—*until you say the words*—isn't there a chance the situation will change? The event will rewind itself, it will never have happened. That final turn Brian didn't make, he will make. He has the will to turn his back on that blinding light that always beckons to the dying in the movies—*Come to the light*. Hell no! *Come back to us.*

Any second now, you will wake up and discover it was all a nightmare. He'll call. It's like he's away on a business trip. You might check your phone for a ping. Not now on your parents' maroon couch with the matching pillows and the news being what it is, *fact*. But, even as you open your mouth to speak the words to your children, you know you'll check your phone the next day—and not just to review every recent text exchange between you and your husband, but to hear, against all common sense, that this was some kind of joke, a Christmas prank, another WTF! situation.

I told our children, "I'm about to tell you the worst news you'll probably ever hear. Daddy died. His plane crashed."

My father, my mother, my sister, and I sat there while, instantly, the kids began repeating: "What? What?"

They began to cry. All of us were crying. Max says now that he started crying because we all were crying—he was so young, he didn't understand.

We hugged and hugged. I don't recall lots of questions at first, only lots of hugs and tears. The firm support of that maroon couch.

The loveseat next to the tree. The sparkle of the tree lights, now blurry in all of our eyes. Eventually, Max would ask, "Can I go play the Wii?" That night, my kids were allowed to do anything they wanted. That night, they could have anything they wanted. Except their daddy walking through the door.

※

After some initial confusion over whom to tell and how to tell it, Mary Kay, Dave, and Donna informed the family, and I called Jen Edstrom, the wife of one of Brian's MIT fraternity brothers. Then I called Tran, Brian's assistant. I called Hillary, my Maryland neighborhood friend. I called Heather, the principal at the kids' school.

Word of the crash spread within minutes—like wildfire across the very social network Brian had helped create—piercing a hole in everyone's sense of security. A brilliant leader and creator, Brian had helped so many people be their best; he had built and been part of so many thriving teams and companies. One of the first companies he founded, Planet All, was the precursor to Friendster, MySpace, LinkedIn, and Facebook. Mark Zuckerberg takes credit for creating the first social network, but he's fooling himself: Brian Robertson created the first social network, and he sold it to Amazon in 1998. When Amazon tells you "Because you liked X, you might like Y," that's Brian Robertson technology.

There are many things people didn't know about Brian, in part because he was modest, and in part because he was doing so much, all the time. Many people knew him, though—he affected many lives. This is why and how the news got out so quickly. Within hours, a couple of our closest friends, Paul and Jigar, hopped in their cars and drove hundreds of miles to be with us. People changed their holiday plans—my friend Alicyn flew thousands of miles—to be with us. My brother Jimmy and his family came to my parents' house immediately.

✳

The night of December 22, nobody wanted to go to sleep. Had it been a "Daddy lands, presents are stuffed in the car, Mommy kisses Santa Claus, and everyone goes a bit crazy hugging, catching up, and eating one more warm cookie" kind of holiday evening, the kids would have been on their way to bed. But, besides Max playing Wii, nobody knew what to do, how to occupy the minutes. Whether to sit or stand or pace or fidget. We were all exposed like actors on stage where the fourth wall has been bashed through. In so many societies, death is a kind of fourth wall—it is the unspoken divide that nobody wants to cross, address, or peer too closely into due to taboo, discomfort, confusion, fear, or being just plain too busy living.

When the veil fell away, though—that membrane that so miraculously and delicately held together everything we knew—we were all terrified of a life without him. I didn't think about this then—I couldn't have—but as word spread among Brian's friends and colleagues, I imagine they felt fear beyond the sadness, too. Confusion. A sense of suddenly not knowing what to do or how to do it.

Though certainly Brian's peers were grown adults, to lose him without warning brought about a loss of innocence on their part, too. We tend to assume our team captain will always be there, but all of a sudden we've got to play one person short and still meet our goals. Many successful enterprises had suddenly lost their visionary get-shit-done center. Dozens of smart entrepreneurs and engineers lost a mentor. The world lost a generous, gifted, hilarious nerd.

Gathering with others and holding them close is a salve for all those feelings we have, at any age, when we're faced with drastic change, with sudden loss. Sadness and all its attendant dark feelings bound together hundreds of people the night of December 22, no matter what holiday they were celebrating, no matter what God and life, death, or rebirth story they were telling. We fear death because what happens afterward is unknown. We fear death because it fucks up our best-laid plans. Death proves we are never in control. After a father, a mentor, a child, or a friend dies, we can never view the world the same way again. Death brings about change, often forced, and most of us are creatures of habit.

We fear death too because of what might happen if and when we begin to feel okay again in the world, despite suffering unfathomable loss.

"I can't live without you," are some of the truest and falsest words ever spoken. The "I" who I was with you, died with you. "Who will I be without you?"

Chapter Six

The kids and I slept together the night of December 22, 2011, in a king-size bed. My parents had recently turned their basement into a bedroom. It was lovely, but, though the space wanted to hold us like a womb that night, it felt like a cold, strange cave. My kids in my arms, my chest sinking and rising in fits and trembles, staring out from my pillow into the darkness where every corner contained the unknown. Above us, you could have heard a sliver of tinsel slide from the Christmas tree. Everyone had gone to bed in the futile attempt to shut the night off, to sleep away the shock, to summon rest enough to make it through the next days.

Mary Kay, who normally would have slept in a room upstairs, stayed close by. She curled up in a blanket on a couch outside our bedroom door in the basement. I could feel her not sleeping, and she could sense me doing the same. In the six months following Brian's death, Mary Kay and I spoke on the phone daily.

Death is a leveler, an equalizer, a primitive thing. In our cave on that king-size bed, my mind ventured into survival mode. I didn't have to ask, "Will the kids and I have enough food, clothing, and shelter?" but "What will we do without Brian?" I'm a strong woman, but I didn't know how to fly without my copilot.

We alternated, that night and into the next morning, between restless and still. Waves of grief start immediately, and when the first wave hit, it knocked me over. I still cannot imagine more pain. In the first hours and days following the worst news of my life, my human body worked in mysterious ways to protect my soul. I walked around in something close to a dream, getting things done but as if I were wearing a suit made of lead.

At first, after a sudden tragic death like Brian's, you ask the simplest questions, often ad nauseam: Why? Why? How? Why?

Before finally dozing off that night, Melanie asked me straight out: "What's going to happen to us? What's going to happen to you? Are you going to be okay, Momma? Are we going to be okay?"

I have no idea how, because I wasn't sure what the next step I needed to take was, but I said, "Yes, we're going to be okay."

Melanie looked at me softly and asked if she could hold my beads.

I was wearing green jasper Mala beads—Buddhist prayer beads—meant to soothe, heal, and protect the heart. I've always, in one form or another, looked for ways to keep my heart strong. Is this because Tricia died of heart complications? Maybe and maybe not, but who do you know that couldn't use a daily boost of peace? The cool green beads always felt satisfying to the touch. Moving them between my fingers would bring back my focus—render me more present, and therefore more alive. Mala beads work for me, and I still have the ones Melanie asked to hold that night.

When the veil falls and we touch the ink-dark abyss or profound joy, or something beyond what we normally know of as real and comforting and existing, the tiniest objects can take on enormous power. A young daughter can become a strong healer, or at least a guide, a maternal figure to her own mother. Melanie held my green Mala beads in one hand that night and stroked my arm with the other.

"We're going to be okay, Momma," she said. "Daddy took care of us. We'll be fine. We've got each other."

The kids and I repeated some version of that *okay* mantra to ourselves and to each other for weeks and months, each of us moving in and out of moments where we really knew and believed it.

※

My children were at an amazing Montessori school at the time. Their teachers, who were highly trained, warm, and nurturing, balanced a full understanding of how children might experience and move through the death of a parent with the business of running a school day to day. Melanie, Brooke, and Max didn't miss a beat in their learning, and teachers didn't miss an opportunity to discuss a tough topic in developmentally appropriate ways. Death—Brian's death—was not ignored or shoved into a corner for the sake of anybody's comfort. This death was part of their learning, and every child who could write at the Montessori Green House wrote my children a sympathy note. In the innocent, direct world of the young, a schoolmate writing to Brooke, "I know exactly how you feel. My kitty died too," contained all the empathy any one of us can ask for.

But Max, because he was so young, had a hard time grasping death. Not that any of us had an easy time working through its implications and reverberations, but how does a young child fully realize they will never again see this person they loved so purely? This consistent, secure, loving guide and presence is "gone." No, they will not be in the audience for your next play or soccer game. No, they won't read you to sleep at night. No, there will be no more flying with Daddy.

After Brian died, Max definitely found darkness. It didn't hit me immediately that his acting out was linked to his own unique processing of losing his father, but telling me he was going to kill himself if I didn't let him eat ice cream was not typical Max behavior, or language. At school, despite the incredible support of teachers and staff, when he got angry or embarrassed, he would flip classroom tables and chairs and say things like, "I'm gonna kill everybody." He was four years old.

We were all angry. Anger, as everyone and their mother knows, is one of the five stages of grief put forward decades ago by psychiatrist Elisabeth Kübler-Ross and death-and-dying guru David Kessler. Originally meant for the dying, but quickly adopted by and for mourners, their model represents a roughly chronological path of grief but is not meant to be prescriptive. There is no "how to grieve" rule book. I went through each stage laid out by Kübler-Ross, and my kids did too. But each stage spiraled and turned and flipped. A stage may seem overcome and surpassed only to reappear out of the blue years later.

No matter how you slice it, grief fits no chart. And super-ugly anger is a super-familiar friend to super-deep sadness. Max was not saying, "I miss Daddy"; he was taking out his longing and rage on tiny chairs.

I was working at the time of Brian's death; I had ten coaching clients, and after he died I kept every one of them. I could have found another coach to take my place—I had the best excuse in the world not to honor my commitments—but the idea of sitting on the couch at home with my sadness was unbearable. Focusing on my entrepreneurial clients and on the wellness company I had recently cofounded took the focus off of me, which was what I needed. Working and feeling like I was making a difference helped me heal.

When I got the call about our table-flipping son, I dropped everything and went to him, thinking, "What the hell am I going to do?" Max and I had been working together with a therapist on what we called his Feeling Book, in which Max drew pictures and I wrote for him words of his own choosing. In a nutshell, this exercise was meant to help him work toward responding "more appropriately" to the perfectly expected and sometimes uncomfortable emotions he was feeling. If he was feeling silly at circle time, he would practice smiling at the teacher instead of dancing around. If he was feeling sad or angry, he could draw a picture or ask to go to the office for a change of scene. The day I left work to help pull him back to center, we ended up sitting together for an hour and a half. I sat through, "I hate you. I hate you. I'm going to throw you over the mountain and I'm going to get my new dad and he'll let me play the Wii."

I told him I would still love him even if he threw me over the mountain.

"I don't want you to love me!" he said.

Those ninety minutes of parenthood were some of the toughest I'd experienced. Max shouted and screamed but he never left the couch. He never got up.

I wondered how long it would go on. I was tempted to tell him that, if he continued to talk this way to me, if he lashed out this way one more time, there would be a time out and he could forget about playing the Wii ever again. Instead, I sat there and loved him. He struggled, but never left my side.

Holy shit, I thought, *so this is how it manifests.* Except for the "new dad" stuff, Max never talked about missing Brian. This was him testing: Can I push mama so far that she'll leave me, too? This was my four-year-old son teaching me in the moment about how to sit in the face of anger and hate that is fueled by sadness and bewilderment. This was Max teaching me directly and intensely about the nature of unconditional love.

＊

On December 23, 2011, my father and brother went to the crash site with the goal of recovering what they could. Brian was Santa—he'd been flying a plane full of presents. The show—Christmas—had to go on. Some sense of normalcy had to play out for the children.

Julie, Brian's sister, had been so excited that year—her family was going to host Christmas Eve dinner and Christmas morning for the first time ever at their new house. But everyone changed plans and gathered at my parents' home first instead: Brian's mother, his father, his sister, and her family arrived the morning of Christmas Eve. We were all in shock and agony together.

The week leading up to Brian's solo cross-country flight had been chaotic. There had been loads of indecisiveness and last-minute logistical mishaps to deal with. When Brian dropped the kids, the dog, and me off at the John Wayne Airport, all seemed as fine as it can seem during holiday travel. But at the check-in counter, the airline representative claimed I had not made a reservation for Cami, our rescue Chihuahua. I called Brian in a mild panic, "Hurry back. You have to come get the dog!"

The kids and I rushed to meet Brian outside of Departures and I handed Cami to him through the passenger side window. We blew each other kisses and said, "I love you!" Brian didn't fly with Cami on the 22nd; he put her in dog camp. Brynn, our amazing babysitter at the time, would end up flying out to my parents' house in the chaos after the crash, dog in tow.

The kids and I made our flight, but by the time we took our seats, I was sweating. That's when Brian sent this text: *I feel really sad we aren't together.*

Really sad.

Brian at one point that week had said, "Maybe I should just hop on a commercial flight, too."

The plane had been loaded with presents a few days before his scheduled departure. The night before the final flight, he texted me several times, irritated because he couldn't find the damn keys to the plane.

Do we know, on a subconscious level, something is different, something is not right? When the universe throws a bunch of kinks in a plan, or at least a few nagging doubts, at what point do we need to listen? Most of the time, there is no drama, no chaos, no trauma and devastation. Thankfully, 90 percent of the time, life plays out pretty much as we expect. It was Christmastime, Brian found the keys to the plane, and the stockings were hung.

The morning of December 22, he called me on his way to the airport. Luckily, I had my phone beside me when I was making waffles for the kids. He sounded happy. He loved flying and was excited about being able to see us that night. We joked about meeting under the mistletoe and ended the conversation with "I love you," and "I love you too."

That next day, when my father and brother left for the York County Airport, I told the kids they could do anything they wanted. I wasn't sure what gifts would be salvageable—could not think in those terms at that moment.

My brother would tell me he could still smell fuel at the crash site. I don't know why that struck or surprised him, or me, but we were all wondering what happened, what happened, what happened?

If I had gone to the crash site, would I want to see more? Would I have been able to resist the urge to look for blood? How much blood was there? I don't know. My brother says it was clear Brian died on impact. Suffered no pain.

I have to believe this.

A story would be printed in the news: An eyewitness told a local reporter that they saw Brian's plane headed directly toward them. They thanked the pilot for making one last turn to land in a field, instead of hitting their house.

One last turn after that one last turn, would he have made it?

They collected Brian's briefcase and luggage. As part of standard operating procedure, the police had already taken his cell phone and iPad. They would search for any aviation information and any "suspicious" communication or browsing history that seemed out of the ordinary. They found nothing. The presence of fuel proved he had not run out of gas. The report from a witness on the ground was that one engine had clearly failed, he could see it was not rotating. I know Brian would not have had any reason to turn off an engine, and I also knew he was trained, as all pilots are, to fly under duress—to fly with one engine if he had to.

He had modified the plane so it could fly at higher altitudes for greater fuel efficiency and to stop quickly for the short field landings we had to make in Mexico and Canada, but everything had been FAA-inspected, certified, and approved. Suffice it to say there would be an investigation into the crash; an official report would be made.

My father and brother laid out the presents they had gathered in the garage. What smelled of fuel, what was broken, what could be rewrapped? I had been crying nonstop on the couch. Talking to people on calls. Sitting with Brian's family. Friends were there, graciously and silently doing anything that had to be done. Brynn was on her way with Cami, our dog. Everyone was falling apart, but not in front of me. Eventually, they asked if I wanted to see the gifts.

Most of the toys, with the exception of—I kid you not—the Barbie Airplane, were intact. Brian and I tried not to spoil our kids, but that Christmas I wanted them to have anything and everything their aching hearts desired. I gave my credit card and the kids' Santa wish lists to my friend Tracey and my brother. I told them, if Mel had eighty toys on her list for Santa, buy her eighty toys. If they saw something they thought Brooke would like, buy it. The sky was the limit for Max, too. All of them.

CHAPTER SEVEN

The most direct route between two points on the surface of a sphere is known as a "great circle." In 2018, Mary Kay and I took off from Chicago and landed in Dublin seven hours later. Did our flight follow the most direct route? I don't know. Multiple factors can cause a pilot to alter his or her course along the way. But we landed, hopped in our rental car, and set out on our sisterly adventure. Mary Kay, perhaps forgetting that the driver's seat was on the left, allowed me, a terrible driver, to take the wheel.

The two of us could not get over the size of the sky in Ireland. Where I currently live, in Chicago, you catch slivers of sky between skyscrapers. You can walk for miles of blocks forgetting that the wind in winter isn't created by the rush of human bodies, that the dog-day heat of August isn't brought on by the swelling masses. Even outside of the city, the Illinois sky is metered out in unimpressive doses. Ireland, in the summer anyway, is a surreal pillow of green set beneath a vivid, vast swath of blue.

Okay, there's white too: white chapels, white sheep, white people.

Everywhere Mary Kay and I looked, we saw ourselves. We met a dozen Marys, Eileens, Patricias, and Mc-Somethings. Irish food, never considered gourmet, we knew too well. Butter! Mom used to put butter on our ham-and-cheese sandwiches, on everything. We had flown to a place so green, so open, so opposite-side-of-the-road, and yet so familiar. At Mr. McGuire's Olde Sweet Shop in Kerry, we bought fudge for everyone back home. On that entire trip, we felt like two little girls in a candy shop. The bubblegum-pink houses with cherry-sorbet-colored doors cheered us. Imagine paint buckets filled with the colors of Kenmare's tiny, tucked-in homes and businesses dumped over the buildings of Chicago, or of your city. Your mood lifts instantly. Ireland is magic.

Ireland is tragic, too. In the mid-nineteenth century, over a million people died in a period of roughly seven years during the Irish Potato Famine, and upward of two million more emigrated in this same stretch of time. The country sustained a loss of nearly a quarter of its population, and the aftereffects were huge and lingering: birth rates dropped, more land fell into the hands of fewer people, and the rift between the Irish and the English grew ever more intense—in part because Irish farmers and peasants were forced throughout the famine to produce and export foods they could not afford.

Everywhere Mary Kay and I walked, we saw statues or plaques reminding us that we were descendants of the Irish stock that left only a few generations ago. Many groups of people—religious, ethnic, and so on—have survived some form of collective and multi-generational hell. Unfortunately, hell is a common place. But something moves through you when you stand in the exact spot where Irish parents sent their children overseas for a chance at a better life, or where a battle covered that same soft valley in blood.

I may not know my deep McGuire history, and I may never find time to research it, but in Ireland I was faced with what extreme struggle and bravery was, and still is, globally. While there, my sister and I talked about feeling grateful for how our parents had raised us: Catholic, engaged weekly in social service, and always ready to help others up a rung. Ireland was key to who we are as a family, and to who I am as a storyteller.

My story began before my parents named me. My name, Eileen, means "the bright one, the shining one;" and though I would never claim to be some magical enlightener, I do know how to hold a light for those who are in the dark. I know how to keep it shining steadily while everything falls apart. Genetically, I am part of a clan that escaped a certain future and ventured into one that was uncertain and unknown. I've got turning hardscrabble to hope in my genes.

In Ireland, Mary Kay and I ate at a place called *Sceal Eile*, Irish for *Another Story*. This is my primary story: I have always refused to be taken down by loss. If I told you that it didn't feel great to feel great again after aching deeply, I'd be lying. I'd be telling you another story—a different one, and it would be fictional. My reality is this: *What story empowers me?* I always try to begin here, eventually, no matter what. We are all victims in some way or another at some point in our lives, and, while there is important work to be done around scarring events and there is fuel in the moment of tragedy and deep pain, repeating a story through the lens of misery, victimhood, and suffering doesn't work for me.

We are also all the victimizer at times. We are the ones that hurt others. We sometimes, intentionally or not, provoke tragedy. The suffering is different but the same. Another story is possible here, too.

Always look inward and look outward. Compassion, forgiveness, gratitude, acceptance, and love will guide our way.

When I am faced with challenges, it is up to me to decide how to interpret them and live through them. "Woe is me" or "life is not fair," in terms of a potential story line, is a dead end. Going through hell allows opportunity for learning and incredible growth. I know that grief is a long haul, and practicing resilience helps. Visiting Ireland, I read and listened to the stories of a massive national trauma and mourning, and I saw that people do rise up and get stronger. Where there is a story of tragedy, there is an opportunity for a story of triumph.

So, I tell my story about losing my sister and my husband in the most authentic way I can. Without authentic stories, we cannot grow. If everything is whitewashed—literally—nothing is added to the human condition. I get thrown back into the dark space of grief now and again, and it will come my way in the future. Losing Brian and Tricia was awful, but I learned that I could use their deaths to find and believe in beauty.

Mary Kay and I have another story—a new one, an additional one—with Tricia now. The trip we took to Ireland was a sisters' trip, and because our baby sister couldn't be there in the flesh, we bought a three-person wooden bench and dedicated it to her. Mary Kay's friends in the small village of Castlelyons hooked us up with the priest of St. Nicholas Church, and this is where Tricia's bench is set.

Twenty-five years ago, we lost her. When the priest blessed her bench, the church bells rang. It was high noon. There were no shadows, only the blue, blue sky above and the green, green grass below.

In Loving Memory of Patricia Ann McGuire. Sitting there, I worried for a moment that nobody would know who Patricia Ann McGuire was. But then I thought about how history and story work in Ireland and decided it didn't matter if nobody knew who my sister was, she was a McGuire. And in Ireland, everyone was connected. Actually, all of us on this great big blue-and-green spinning circle are bound to one another—we are one—so whoever sits on my sister's bench will lovingly remember someone.

✳

Mary Kay and I happened to be visiting Ireland during a record heat wave and the region's worst drought in decades. Roads literally melted; water was rationed. Livestock farmers worried about inflated hay prices come fall and winter; people chatted in pubs about climate change. Across the Emerald Isle, as Mary Kay and I were marveling at the vast blue sky and ubiquity of butter in County Cork, photographers were taking aerial photos of parched yellowed forests and scorched fields of grass.

Evidence of climate change is being recorded in every corner of the world. Increasingly, there is no escaping it. And while none of it is easy to reconcile, and many wonder if we're doing too little too late, there was beauty to be found in some of the images of the heat-swept British Isles: The landscape revealed stunning, rarely seen sub-terranean tracings of historic and prehistoric archaeological features.

These "ghosts" of ruins aren't visible under usual weather and farming conditions; but in July 2018, a never before seen "new Stone-henge" was discovered by a drone pilot within a mile of the 5,000-year-old Neolithic tomb Newgrange. The owner of the drone, who runs the website *Mythical Ireland*, told reporters that he and his work partner were "very giddy" when they realized the significance of their find.

Mary Kay and I didn't visit Newgrange, but I've since learned a bit about Irish tombs and mythology. Newgrange is one of several earth and stone monuments that make up the Brú Na Bóinne Complex, a UNESCO World Heritage Site. It is an impressively large mound: approximately 279 feet wide and 45 feet tall, it covers more than one square acre of normally lush green land. Neolithic farmers hauled rock and stone slabs directly from the Boyne River and from up to fifty kilometers away—probably over several decades—to build the structure.

Originally, Newgrange was thought to be primarily a tomb, due to the ancient human remains found there; now historians and archaeologists believe the monument also served as a place of ritual, or for community gatherings. Magically—magnificently—this mon-ument captures the sunrise of the Winter Solstice. Each year around December 22, *if* the mists have cleared over Ireland, a long ray of sun enters a window-like feature called a "roofbox" and moves down the

60-foot-long interior passageway of Newgrange until it fully illuminates the bones and ashes of the dead at the center.

It's easy to understand why the builders and pilgrims of Newgrange wanted to capture, honor, and worship the sun. Their lives depended on knowing the sun intimately. They were farmers. Their building of mounds, henges, and stone circles might have been completely practical, but I doubt it.

I wonder if the light landing on the bones of ancestors brings the dead back for a brief spell. For those who say the dead can't be summoned, if the people gathering to raise them believe in what they are doing, does proving them wrong (or primitive, or woo-woo) matter?

Some believe the chambers inside these Neolithic mounds are where the cult of the dead worshipped. Deep in the interior of these spaces decorated with spirals, dots, and parallel lines, the Otherworld could be accessed. The Otherworld, in some Irish tales, is where the dead and the gods play. In other stories, it is the realm of beauty, abundance, joy, health, and youth everlasting. Who wouldn't want to get down on their knees and pray, or let it all go in dance and give thanks to those who guard it?

The ancient Celts believed the Otherworld exists alongside our own. There are moments when the Otherworld can permeate this world we consider ours. There are liminal instances and spaces, parallel universes, colors and objects and energies our eyes simply are not built to see. But if we slow down, breathe, believe a little in the mystical, we might be able to *sense*, if not *see* them. Some of us have experienced time moving differently, a draft passing behind us and making the hair on the back of our necks stand up.

I have always believed my angels are with me, and after visiting Ireland with Mary Kay, I feel less kooky saying it out loud. I'm as practical and as logical as a person can be. But the Irish in me and maybe the Irish Catholic does believe in miracles, mysteries, fairies, praising the light, and bringing light to the dead.

Most important, though, I believe in bringing light to those who outlive the dead.

In the middle of our darkest hours, how can any of us capture or receive that rare ray of sunshine, that warm reassurance? It seems to me our ancient ancestors knew part of the answer: Create space. Allow stillness. Come together. Honor our dead and the realm we do not know. Understand that a rare glimpse of hope can be the start of a major shift—a new season. Listen, share stories, tell your truth, and trust in cycles and in something larger. Trust the universe.

✳

In his book *The Celtic Twilight*, the Irish poet William Butler Yeats wrote, "In Ireland, this world and the world we go to after death are not far apart." I find comfort in these words, but more important, truth—a truth that fits with mine. Brian and Tricia are close by.

James Joyce's novella, *The Dead,* explores the role of the dead in the lives of those who survived them. Immediately following the deaths of my sister and my husband, it wasn't possible to know how and where they would remain part of me, and one thing I definitely didn't want to hear was "They'd want you to be happy and move on." But, of course, it was true, and eventually I found larger and more solid handholds to grab on to when attempting to haul myself up and over the cold, hard mountain of grief. I had to process my sister Tricia's death when I was in my early twenties, and though I had tremendous support from family and friends, I still had to find the tools that worked best for me. I had to sit in my own dark space, pay attention to anything and everything that felt good to me, and make the journey on my own. The same was true after Brian's death. I didn't "get better" at grieving because I had done it before. But I did know things would get better.

Those of us granted the gift of living have work to do, adventures to take, light to share. Are the promises made to a sister, brother, mother, father, spouse, friend, or child broken when the amazingly complex body that houses spirit ceases to function and be? I think it is up to us to choose.

One promise—spoken or not—that many of us make to a loved one is that we will do our best. Other promises might be these: We will lay our beloved to rest in accordance with their wishes. We will keep learning. We will attempt to engage in work fueled by passion. We will raise our children according to shared expectations, visions, and dreams. We will never give up.

But even with that promise, tragedy often calls for a change— usually something has to give. Brian would understand that the company I was set to help launch before he died had to go on without me. For six months into 2012, I did try to consult with my business partners. I fought to stay present and to contribute to the growth of a stellar company that was centered on corporate health and wellness, but my family's health and wellness needed to come first.

After the plane crash, I gave myself a time out. Brian, I know, would not have had a problem with my doing this, as long as I respected the time. Half of our Power Duo was gone, and now I had to figure out how to draw on my own power, function solo, and make my life matter. Right after Brian's death, when I finally found the energy to get off my parents' couch and take a shower, I stood for a long time under the water. They say water is a conduit to spirit: the other side can find you there. Behind the locked door and shower curtain, I could cry. I could be vulnerable, in no rush to feel anything but warmth.

"Oh, my God," I was sobbing. "I can't do this alone. I'm not strong enough to do this by myself."

And then I swear I heard Brian say something like, "That one was a little pathetic."

It wasn't his voice, but I knew it was him, and he was right. I felt the connection and it made me smile. It seemed that one of Brian's roles would be continuing to make me smile.

"You're right," I said aloud. "It's pathetic to think I can't do this. I can and I will. But still, it really sucks that you're gone."

CHAPTER EIGHT

On our sisters' trip to Ireland, I learned more about my roots than I had expected. Mary Kay and I went with the intention to honor a family tie cut too soon, but it wasn't in my mind to be taken any further back in time. Silly, I suppose, since much of the Emerald Isle seems to be cut of another era.

When the sun rises in Ireland on December 22, I discovered, it casts light on bones and ashes that are stored in the inner chamber of Newgrange. Brian died on the Winter Solstice. Am I crazy to think this world is full of wonder, and to make this connection? What role does my Irish heritage play in the fact that I feel lucky?

Brian and I had found one another; we were lucky. Both of us had been born lucky, really, in that we had caring and committed parents who valued family, hard work, and education. Brian was raised by two teachers who are wicked smart and down-to-earth. He attended school in a town of 1,600, two hours north of Toronto. He excelled at geekery in his early years, winning the Canadian National Science Fair with an exhibit on rocketry. He was a water-sport nut, too: At age seventeen, he was the barefoot waterskiing champion of Canada. And then he attended MIT and Harvard. Not all rural kids find and take the route Brian did.

Brian was lucky: His parents channeled the brains and energy he was born with and gave him opportunities to excel. David, Brian's father, is one of the funniest men on the planet—his humor ran through his son's veins, and I find it popping up now, all the time, in our kids.

I could always see the boy in Brian, and I see Brian in Max. How does this nature/nurture thing work? Brian had only four short years to influence our son. Their shared gestures and attitudes are bewildering and comforting.

Brian accomplished more professionally by age thirty-eight than most people do in multiple lifetimes, and yet at home, around me and our children, he could be an absolute nut. I don't think anyone outside of family and his closest crew knew how funny he was. He did a Beavis and Butthead imitation I can still hear. He danced in his underwear and knee-high Gold Toe socks in the morning. He was lucky, successful, and happy.

As a kid—even before he was a kid—did he know that his time on Earth would be limited? He was exceptional about time. He utilized every minute. On December 22, he was meant to land at 5:32 p.m., but told me to pick him up at 6:00 because he didn't want me waiting around. My time, my twenty-eight minutes, mattered to him. And at 6:00 on the dot, we would have been all in.

At Brian's funeral, so many people spoke about being grateful for the time he had spent with them. I marveled at this at first, because Brian was such a fierce guardian of his time. But then I got it, after not just five people expressed gratitude, but literally hundreds. At the funeral I wasn't able to process much, but a few words stuck with me, and I would hear them again and again in the months following his death: *When Brian gave you ten minutes, he really gave you ten minutes. He was fully present. His way of being changed the course of my life.*

Being present made Brian more efficient and effective than most people. The speed with which he could process complex concepts and take action constantly boggled my mind. I heard from more than one of his peers, "Brian would be the first person I'd hear from in the morning and the last person to send an email at night." He never went to bed with a full email inbox; he typed faster than most professional typists. Before the kids could read, he had plans to teach them to speed-read.

His need for speed was part of our relationship. When I first met Brian, I felt like I had jumped on a fast train, and I never looked back. We were together a total of fourteen years, and between various internships, jobs, and schooling, we moved eleven times. It was exhilarating as hell. One time, Brian was debating buying a building at auction. I was in exercise class, blissfully jamming away. When I checked my phone afterward, I saw that he'd called me over a dozen times. *Call me, call me. There's this building for sale.* He'd wanted my input. And then, before my exercise class was over, he had bought it.

That building became the first office of SunEdison—a solar company Brian cofounded at the beginning of his eight-year solar energy career. His dedication to alternative energy was born out of the necessity to power our place in a fairly remote part of Mexico. I was determined that his vision would not die when he did.

Brian was a guy who loved and launched rockets; talked physics, economics, world politics, computer code, and engineering; and yet still wrote everything down on a yellow notepad. Someday, far off in the future, I can see a team of archaeologists unearthing a box of pages and pages of his To Do lists. They'll wonder if it was the work of a man or a machine. Brian *was* a machine, and how he stayed so joyful in the midst of all of his accomplishments and their accompanying obligations remains a mystery to me. He had visions for what he wanted to create; he thought big and believed he could do anything.

As his partner, I'd sometimes crack up: "You actually think you can do it? I think you can do it. Everyone else thinks you can do it. But do they know how silly you are, too?"

Every day, Brian woke up happy. This is not fiction or me remembering a world through rose-colored lenses. It's a simple fact.

✳

In the spectrum of pessimism to optimism, I certainly have enough "excuses" to be mad, to whine, to ask the universe, "Why me? Why did you take Tricia? Brian? My dear friend Nina?" I could repeat to others, "Life is unfair."

The English translation of the Gaelic *Mag Argatnél* is "the silver-cloud plain." Mag Argatnél is the Otherworld. Joy is abundant in the Otherworld, and if you believe this plane we inhabit and define as the land of the living does touch gently against the land of gods, the dead, and everlasting youth—or immortality—grab as much joy as you can.

Laugh, and laugh at yourself. Brian once mistook dog treats for beef jerky. Another time, I caught him spitting something out into his hand. "What's wrong?" I asked. He had evidently been hungry.

"Don't tell your mom, but her snacks are stale."

"That's potpourri!" I said.

Wow, how such ridiculous moments can make up a great life!

I could spend the rest of my years (or days) stuck in *what if* and *only if*, but, *Sceal Eile*, I choose the happy story. Maybe not right away. With tragedy or trauma, at first, we don't know what is happening or why. We're in a fog, and that's okay. How to start healing is a mystery. In ancient Irish mythology, the deities moved among us mere mortals cloaked in a magic mist that rendered them invisible. What if, in some of our most confusing moments, we are surrounded by supernatural beings, gods, goddesses? When normal conditions cease to be, what comes into relief might have value, beauty, lessons.

And when the fog or the mist begins to give way to moments of clarity, when the rain comes after a long drought, if we resign ourselves to the fact that we are not in control, we can be freed. We can let this life—dark, shadowy, brilliant, and hilarious—unfold. We can want to feel okay again. Then great. We can accept that more straight-up hell will come around, and it will never get easier, but each time we survive it, we'll learn. We have an endless capacity to start over again, fly again, and love.

CHAPTER NINE

One of the biggest tragedies to me about Brian's death is that he was firing on all cylinders. He was finally an "adult." His ego had grown up. The impatient sock-it-to-ya buzz of his twenties had mellowed a bit as he moved into his thirties. From building his first internet company in the 1990s, to his work with Amazon, Visible Markets, and the solar industry, he had learned, taken risks, and done lots of the deep work of transforming. He was in a groove and poised to make a huge difference in the field of energy and the environment.

And then BAM. He left hundreds of people spinning: *What?! Now what?*

The day after the crash, December 23, 2011, certain things needed to be done. My parents connected with people at their church to begin funeral arrangements as my brother and father went out to the crash site to see what they could see, to recover the recoverable.

Despite the level of financial planning Brian had done—and I'm hoping here that readers will read between the lines and start having some of those uncomfortable conversations about end-of-life preparations, wills, and estates—I was dismayed at how bureaucratic the process of settling our affairs was. Obviously, I'd never had to deal with my husband dying before, and the legalese was mind-boggling. In my most fragile state, being asked to read the small print could have been salt on the wound; but I signed and initialed one form after the other, because that was what I was told I had to do.

When a person dies, their bank accounts are frozen, and you have no idea how long they'll stay that way. If you are fortunate enough to have life insurance, or to have thought of setting it up before it's too late, there is no guarantee as to when you'll receive your money. Because most of our bank accounts were in Brian's name, I needed to transfer money quickly to make sure the kids and I would be okay. I needed money in my account to pay the bills.

It was nuts. On December 26, puffy-eyed, parched, and in pain, I was driving back from the mall, where we had just bought Max new shoes for his daddy's funeral. This was back in the days before ubiquitous Wi-Fi access, and I had my dad on my cellphone. He was on his home computer conferencing with me and the people at my bank. Bankers can't simply follow orders from even a grieving woman's father, so there I was, granting everyone permission to do this and that, and telling my father our password.

"That's not it," my dad said. "Invalid password."

I'm driving, I'm drained, but I'm sure of our damn bank password. "Try it again."

My dad enters our password several times before he finally gets it right.

The pressure on him, when I think about it now, was funny as hell. And me, looking like I had been at Santa's workshop pulling fifteen-hour graveyard shifts and barking into the phone: "Make sure

CAPS LOCK isn't on!" and thinking, "Don't lock us out, Dad. Please, don't fuck this up!"

*

Because of the number of people Brian knew and the time of the year, it was decided immediately that there would be more than one memorial service. His employees in California told me I would not have to lift a finger for the West Coast ceremony—they would plan and manage everything. I accepted their generosity. Brian's parents would hold a ceremony in Canada. I understood their need to honor their son where they had raised him.

My parents, in contacting their church to begin making funeral arrangements, did what nobody else was capable of doing. I was grateful to them for taking immediate action, immediate control. But, while my father and brother were out at the airport picking through the pieces of Brian's plane, airport staff relayed a message: A man named Al Khuner from the local Khuner Associates Funeral Home wanted to know if he could get in touch with me.

When my brother came home and told me this, my initial reaction was to question why a funeral home owner was reaching out to me. I was skeptical, thinking he must be an ambulance chaser. My mom and dad had things covered; but at my brother's urging, thankfully and miraculously, I returned Al's call.

Al Khuner, also a pilot, had been flying the same flight pattern as Brian the night of December 22. He had heard Brian over the radio, communicating with the NTSB. (York Airport is an unmanned airport; there is no flight tower.)

"I landed thirty minutes before Brian was supposed to," he told me on the phone.

My heart, if it was out of steam at that time, must have leapt. My heart, if it was beating too fast that hour, must have calmed.

"I would be honored," Al said, "as pilot to pilot, to take care of all your husband's funeral expenses."

What kind of stranger makes this kind of offer? I wondered.

My second thought was the answer: An angel.

With gratitude and an instinctual confidence that the funeral would be perfect in Al's hands, I let go.

"Okay," I said.

If changing funeral arrangements on a whim upset my parents or their church friends, I don't know. I doubt it did, but either way, in my state of trauma, I knew that I had to go with what felt right to me. Even in chaos, there are moments where you know beyond doubt that if you let anyone else dictate or contradict matters of your heart, you will live to regret it. In the immediate hours and days following the crash, as unclear and rudderless as I felt at the time, I was going with the flow. Here was a man, a pilot, who had heard Brian's voice—disconnected, floating out there in the ether of that dark December airspace. He had heard Brian speak the words, "Engine out." He might have heard Brian's very last word, which would have been "Mayday."

Al and I quickly determined that his funeral home, though

large, wouldn't be spacious enough for all the people who wanted to come to the East Coast memorial service to bid Brian Robertson farewell. Also, there was no major airport nearby, and people were going to fly in from around the world. I suggested to Al we hold the wake at his beautiful funeral home and the memorial service in Baltimore, between where Brian's sister lived and where he and I had lived.

"I'd like a gorgeous space," I said. "Like a museum."

Al knew a caterer in Baltimore who knew the city like no other and would deliver us a few options. Until everyone got through Christmas, though, there was nothing to be done—nobody was working anywhere. Between the plane crash on the night of the 22nd and the visit to the mall for funeral shoes on the 26th, my family and Brian's family did our best to keep the holiday spirit alive. And then, on December 27 and 28, Al and the universe led me somehow in the planning of Brian's funeral and the first of his three life celebrations.

On the phone with the caterer, I Googled the places she named as possibly suitable for Brian's memorial service. I clicked through several fingernail images, instantly rejecting the ones I didn't love. When she suggested the Alonzo G. Decker Gallery at the Baltimore Museum of Industry, I zoomed in and enlarged the image once, then twice, and then a third time. I couldn't believe my eyes.

"This is it," I told her. This was one of many "but of course" moments to come.

The Decker Gallery was perfect: A twin-engine plane hung from the ceiling, and light poured in through floor-to-ceiling windows that looked out on Baltimore's Inner Harbor. The space accommodated three hundred people. The fact that it was housed in the Baltimore Museum of Industry was no coincidence—innovation and industry were Brian's middle names.

Al took me under his wing, and the amazing thing was, I let him. When you are trudging through foreign territory and trying to plan the kind of event you don't expect to have to plan until you are retired and wrinkled, leaning on people who know what they are doing helps ease the pain. Never one to like feeling out of control, I completely surrendered when Brian died. I had to.

My husband's death was a huge opportunity for me to wise up to the reality that none of us is in control of everything. Something larger than us and larger than the sum of us is always present, and it does—at times—take over. Tragedy illuminates our need to exhale and give in; but ever since Brian's death, I have tried to be more conscious of when and where I still need to step more gracefully toward surrender and support.

After Brian's funeral in Baltimore, I would tell Al, "You are literally a live angel to me. You are so good at your job. You have found your calling."

Prior to the funeral, on Christmas Eve of all evenings, everyone but Mary Kay and the kids accompanied me to the Khuner Funeral Home to start planning Brian's memorial. After introductions and condolences, Al pulled me aside. From the get-go, he made it clear that, though many beloved mourners were present, I would be "the decider." As he led me alone to the casket showroom, a part of my heart was crying out, "Mayday! Mayday!" and another was shouting,

"How do I pick out a box to put my husband's body in? Who gives a fuck about this box?!"

It was a horrible, bizarre moment—casket shopping is not car shopping, and this was a task I had never envisioned. But I knew that, though we were going to have Brian cremated and this box would be temporary, we were having an open casket at his funeral. I would do what I had been doing since the moment I pulled up to the York Airport and my entire reality had shattered. I would do what Brian and I had been trained to do, more or less, in all of our transformational work together. I would do what felt right in the moment, moment-by-moment. I chose a nice wooden casket with a silky white interior.

Al was a gentle and efficient pro. I told him I couldn't imagine anyone better than a pilot to help me start the surreal process of saying goodbye to a pilot. "We're a unique breed," he said. He offered comfort, too, in saying what others would say, and which was true: "Brian died doing what he loved." Brian loved doing so many things, but yes, he died while living a childhood dream he'd made real. No regrets.

"I want you to know you'll hear things," Al said. "It doesn't matter what happened in the sky, NTSB will tell you it was the pilot's fault."

He was right about what the NTSB would tell us, but at that point, of course, we didn't know anything. We were all still completely immersed in *what happened what happened what happened* mode—trying to answer this question for people, with no answers yet for ourselves.

In the long and sometimes eternal limbo of not knowing—of wanting to know, and of not wanting to know—you eventually stop wishing you could turn back time, and you start trying to make sense of things. Logic slaps you relentlessly to attention until you concede that a respectable portion of pain consists of you arguing with reality and losing. At first, my urge to know what happened in Brian's last moments wasn't gut-wrenching, it was gut-punching; I wanted to know that the crash, and his death, were not his fault. In pressing the universe and anyone in it who might have answers, though, I kept falling into endlessly looping black holes of knowing about unknowing: Having the answers wouldn't make a difference; answers would not stop the pain.

For months, I would work through dozens of iterations of possible details and likely scenarios, knowing that, despite the thorough investigation that was to come, we would likely never get a perfect replay of how or why N48BS went down.

I knew this too, for a fact: Brian's energy had passed through me while I sat at the York Airport waiting for the answer I dreaded most, and, after that answer was delivered, all other answers held less power.

In the days immediately following Brian's death, in those first moments where I had a taste of what our relationship would look like moving forward, his energy would pierce through my sadness. I wondered if I was going crazy. *You are being taken care of, Eileen.* In that first shower I took after his death, I sensed he was still with me, and this feeling simultaneously freaked me out and calmed me. Brian had not abandoned me; he was still loving me; he was still talking to me and pulling strings with the collective conscious universe. Knowing his energy hadn't simply been wiped off the face of the earth comforted me.

I thought that Brian, wherever he had gone, might be asking why, too—might now be stepping into an entirely new sea of mysteries and wonders. I wanted to ask him what it was like "over there." Not that I wanted to die too—I didn't—but I wanted to be with him. We had always been excellent traveling companions, and, though I knew I was being irrational, I was slightly jealous he was taking such a monumental adventure solo. He had been an avid explorer and learner, so what would become clear to him there, on the other side? I wanted to know; I wanted to know what Brian knew.

They say humans can perceive only 4 percent of the universe— I have always wanted access to more. My tears decades ago on the flight to Phoenix were tears of all the joy in possibility. To think that, from this limited field of perception, we each craft entirely different stories and unique realities intrigues and excites me. Had the kids and I been on the plane with Brian, and had we crashed but all survived, each of us would have painted a different picture of falling from the sky. The answers to the question, "What happened?" would vary. To me, these differences in perception, imagination, and reality are not confusing, not right or wrong, but proof that anything is possible—proof that the sky is *not* the limit.

I wanted to know what had happened to Brian in that plane, but I didn't. I wondered: if I were to learn that Brian had made a mistake, would I feel mad at him? I tackled questions I didn't want to whisper aloud, and eventually realized that I would write the story of our lives together, the way each of us writes our own life story. Each of us is trying to make sense of things—from the silliest events and challenges to the toughest—by weaving together facts and feelings we can live with. Most of us never have all the pieces we need to complete the puzzle and we choose the pieces that best suit our needs, hopes, and desires.

My survival strategy after Brian died was to continually choose what felt best for me and for our children. Pain highlights where there is difficult work to do, and I try hard not to run away from it. But it also worked for me to lean toward what felt good and light and positive as often as I could. My husband, a man who literally harnessed the sun for a living, died on the darkest night of the year. The kids and I survived our darkest night; we are alive because we have work to do and light to share.

CHAPTER TEN

When a loved one is sick for a prolonged period of time, when they are dying—*in the present progressive verb tense*—there is time to research end-of-life options and time for the person who is in the process of departing to discuss these options with the people who will be left behind. This doesn't mean a slow, predictable death is easier, but it does mean there is time to make all sorts of arrangements and amends. When someone dies out of the blue, you aren't prepared for anything. Everything happens fast as fuck!

When it came time to see Brian's body, the day before the funeral on December 29, Al first sat with us. He told us, "He's not going to look like he did when he was alive. We put a lot of makeup on him." Melanie and Brooke, young and confused, giggled nervously at the thought of makeup on Daddy.

I smiled. What do you say? Nervous laughter is common; Brian wearing makeup was certainly not. I told the kids their dad probably had some bruises, like anyone would after falling, and that Al had covered them nicely. Within days, I was ad-libbing, freestyling, trying to explain death on children's terms, trying to help them understand that it's true we all die, and it's also true no one should have to bury a thirty-eight-year-old man in the prime of his life.

Kids, we can't control a thing, but don't worry, I won't die suddenly too. Really? How can I promise that? What the hell with these polarities?

The notion of seeing Brian's lifeless body was crushing. I wanted to vomit. I had never been more nervous in my life.

Once again, though, Al took me first and alone to the room with the casket. Al walks widows and widowers to the sides of caskets for a living, and he's good at it. At the casket, he asked if I wanted Brian's ring. I said, "Yes." I took off my rings and then slid his ring—which was big on me—onto my ring finger, closest to my heart. As soon as I placed my rings back on top of his, a transformation took place: I was marrying Brian all over again.

I know I wasn't breathing because I remember telling myself, "Breathe, Eileen. You've got to breathe." I managed a deep breath. Brian didn't look like himself; he looked like he'd lost twenty pounds. I took another deep breath. He looked at peace. Once I was inhaling and exhaling like a living human being, I reached out. The moment I touched his hand, the recognition struck me that all of us are, foremost, spiritual beings, temporarily living this human experience. How could I have forgotten our bodies are mere containers? Brian had become a casing. His fingers were cold and rocklike, while mine were burning, weightless, nothing.

Our souls fill these bodies of ours with energy, our breath moves in and out of our lungs, we take up space and make our voices heard, and then—*poof!* Brian, as I knew him, was no longer in that room. He was not in his body—that body. His light had flown.

Al gave me all the time I needed, and in that time, with our rings stacked in their new arrangement, I promised Brian I would do every-thing that we had promised each other we were going to do. I told him, "I'm going to be okay. You're going to be okay. You take it from your side and I'll take it from this one. We've got this."

For the most part, I meant I would raise the kids as we had planned, but I also meant I was going to reach for a goal that Brian had not supported because it would have encroached on family time. Clearly, almost defiantly, in that room, I told him I was going to train to be a yoga teacher. Training would keep me breathing and would teach me how to help others breathe as well.

I did end up getting my yoga teaching certificate, and I still teach on and off. When Brian died, pieces of me did, too. Practicing daily intensive breath work fed my heart the oxygen it needed to regrow. Being present on my yoga mat was the most comfortable place for me to be—the past was devastating and a future without Brian was, too. Eventually, memories of him would become a com-fort, but in those first months in child's pose or warrior pose, I wanted nothing to interrupt the present moment—the now. In yoga, I could control my breathing and time.

After assuring Brian that everything and everybody would be okay, for humor's sake, I put a Blackberry in his hand. I didn't know where he was or what he was doing, but I was sure that one habit he would never escape was his use of technology to organize, network, and hustle.

When Al brought everyone else in—my side and Brian's side of our family—the kids asked if they could touch their daddy. They commented on his makeup. They said their daddy didn't look like himself. There were tears. When Brooke asked if she could do a cartwheel, we let her do a cartwheel—it lightened things up. I don't know what the kids were thinking, I don't know what anyone was thinking, and I don't know that I was thinking anything beyond the fact that we would have an open casket at the wake because I wanted to be with Brian's body every single second I still could.

Mistakenly, for me, I had chosen not to see Tricia's body after she died. I learned then that you're only given one chance to see someone for the last time.

A few days later, at the end of the wake, Dave and Donna would be the last to lay eyes on Brian. Their love had created him. They were the first to see him as he entered this world, and there they were, doing the one thing parents are not supposed to do—saying their last goodbye to their child.

*

How in the hell do you plan a memorial for your thirty-eight-year-old spouse? Everyone was giving me space, but at the same time they were looking to me to make all these decisions. At first, from my parents' couch with my head pounding and my eyes constantly burning with tears, I couldn't handle it. How could I be the one expected to decide on funeral stuff?

I always liked to make all the decisions, to be in control. My father used to tease me that I'd call him for advice, and he would toss options at me until I heard the one I wanted to hear. He finally learned, when I would ask for advice, to say, "What answer do you want me to give you?" But now I was in surrender mode. Al was my guide and it was his job to field and direct all funeral-related questions to me.

Fairly quickly, I snapped out of one surreal state of being, only to land in another. "Brian's my husband. I'm *the one*. It's up to me to make the call."

I felt like a creature amped on a billion volts of adrenaline. Coffee? I couldn't. Beer or wine, I wouldn't drink for months. Instinctively, I knew three things: I had to stay healthy to stay strong; I had to go straight at the pain and not dull it; and I was going to give Brian the freaking memorial of a lifetime. I was going to throw him a ceremony he'd wish he could attend.

My biggest concern in giving Brian the best going-away party of his life was our children. I didn't want to hurt anyone's feelings, but I also didn't want a low-key traditional memorial service where two or three people read poems or sang, and one person gave the eulogy. The End.

Not good enough for Brian.

I have no clue where I got the idea, but I decided that, at Brian's service, we'd go Quaker open-mic style. Anyone and everyone who had something to say could say it. If hundreds of us stayed in that Alonzo G. Decker Gallery at the BMI until it closed, we would. Seventeen people ended up standing and talking about Brian in Baltimore. Sam Choi was one of them.

Sam, his fraternity brother at MIT and cofounder and partner from Visible Market days, joked about Brian becoming a waterskiing champion in Canada, a country "so cold, that ice melts to water only seven days a year." On a more serious note, he acknowledged what I, so intimately, had been recognizing and feeling, that Brian's emotional IQ had caught up to his intellectual IQ, and he was firing on even more cylinders than ever before.

Sam closed by saying:

> "In American history, very few people are known first and foremost by their three initials. I can think of LBJ, FDR, JFK, and MLK. MLK, by the way, passed away at the tender age of thirty-nine. And even more ironically, JFK's son, JFK Jr., passed away when he was BDR's age, thirty-eight and also in a private plane crash. Our BDR dies with his three-initial moniker intact. BDR went to MIT and became CEO. B D R, R I P."

A few days later, in Huntington Beach, another MIT friend of Brian's, Shane Crotty, who is now curing cancer, spoke about the time Brian bested him in the election for fraternity president, even though Brian wasn't in town—he was abroad, studying in Russia—during the campaign.

✳

In the days leading up to Brian's East and West Coast memorial services, I would experience surges of energy fueled by remembrances of Brian's humility. Brian was as comfortable with politicians and dignitaries as he was with his best friends. Among the thousands of condolences we would receive over the next month was a card from former Vice President Al Gore. He and Brian had met because of Brian's leadership role in the solar industry, and Mr. Gore had been in a position in 1998 to grant him an extended stay on his work visa, in the form of a National Interest Waiver. Yes, it was literally in the best interests of the United States to let the brainy Canadian guy stay.

People who didn't know him very well told me after the memorial service they had attended that they were grateful to have crossed paths with him, and were blown away to learn of his list of accomplishments. "He never told us any of this stuff," they said.

I knew that the other dads from his Indian Princess tribe—a father-daughter YMCA organization—had no idea Brian met with the prince of Saudi Arabia to work on a solar energy plan for the country. Brian had always simply shown up to do Indian Princess things like fill water balloons with the girls and drink a beer with the men. If he'd just flown in from a day-long meeting in China, where he had appeared on national Chinese television, he would change outfits in the car, going from Superman (in expandable-waisted pants) to Clark Kent in two minutes. Because he was so humble, I decided, his memorials would be his coming-out party.

The world needed to know what we lost. Our kids needed to know. I needed to capture this.

Maybe everyone feels this way, maybe not, but I needed to step up. I wanted to look nice; I wanted to make Brian proud. Getting out of bed or off the couch was not easy, but at some point in those final days of December 2011, I got the hell up and then barely sat down. It was time to throw the best celebration of a life anyone had ever seen, for the man I—and so many others—loved, cherished, and admired.

This was *it* for Brian.

As soon as I turned toward the joy this remembrance could be, crazy things started happening, synchronicities, things to which Brian would have said, "Hell, yes!" We'd always had moments where we felt simultaneously plugged directly into the universe. We'd smile, knowing we were lucky. We knew how lucky we were, and damn if Brian wasn't helping me plan the Baltimore gathering, by saying, *Keep saying yes, Eileen. Surrender. We've got this.*

The caterer presented me with a list of foods: Would we like clam chowder and bacon-wrapped scallops? Yes, we would, those were Brian's favorite things to eat. In the shower I thought, "We need to kick off this party with our friend Joe singing." I called him, and to our surprise, neither of us remembered what song he had sung at our wedding. Thirty minutes later he called back: "Eileen," he said. "It was 'We Live on Borrowed Time.'"

Yes, of course!

What the final song would be in Baltimore, we didn't know yet, but in the meantime, I had to write my own song for Brian—his eulogy, an elegy, a thank-you and farewell. I was stumped. I didn't know where to begin or how to avoid all the clichés about life and death, when clichés could never capture his.

I didn't consider myself a writer, but I had a severe case of writer's block. The morning of December 27, after the predictable tossing and turning, I woke up with a jolt. Humor, start there!

"He was constantly whistling and singing to himself in the morning. I'd come into the bathroom and he'd be standing in his underwear with his lucky Gold Toe socks pulled all the way up to his knees, singing, 'I'm too sexy for my socks, too sexy for my socks . . .'"

Brian was silly, fun, and hilarious. But what else would inspire the people who had come to honor him? How could my spoken words mirror the words Joe would sing, in a way that might gently nudge everyone present to wake up, step out of their comfort zones or illusions of security, and live more in consonance with the finite number of precious days we've been granted?

Brian did so much, he made many contributions, he had infinite ways of asserting himself in and responding to the world. My fingers couldn't keep up with my thoughts—I'd write a sentence or two and crumple up the paper. I'd rewrite sentences, and when I got goose-bumps, I knew that I had nailed it. I was in the flow. These words that were being handed to me—by another consciousness, by Brian?—would soar from the page to the hearts of a room full of devastated people. I wasn't claiming to be Shakespeare, or even a writer, but I could sense that a word or phrase or truth might stick with one colleague, another with a wife, and another with a child.

"The Number One reason I loved Brian: He was committed to making a difference in the world, in big and in small ways. My honey was on an unstoppable mission, which I believe began when he started carrying a briefcase to school at age six . . . .

"In the months before he died, he was traveling around the world, meeting in palaces and with highpowered executives in countries like India, China, Saudi Arabia, Mexico, and Italy. He was creating plans to change how the world harnesses energy, and was having a positive impact on our environment and the planet . . . .

"My request and my invitation to you is to spend the rest of your borrowed time making a difference in the world—this can be as simple as staying up too late on a school night to talk to your children, or as complicated as curing cancer . . . ."

From Baltimore, to Huntington Beach, to the service in Canada eight months later—I would feel immense love pouring from each guest's heart. When someone stood to speak about Brian, no one else said a word. Whether I'd heard a story a dozen times from one of his amazing fraternity brothers, or a colleague was delivering words of praise I wouldn't have been able to drum up myself, I was riveted.

And the song we finally chose to close Brian's first memorial service?

While Mary Kay was driving Melanie, Brooke, Max, and me to the Baltimore Museum of Industry on that strange, surreal day, Adele's "Someone like You" came on the car radio. My sister and I exchanged glances—Bingo!

※

The kids and I walked into the Decker Gallery looking the best we could. Of course, we had not flown to my parents' house that Christmas prepared for a funeral. Our suitcases were packed with flannel pajamas, comfy pants, and hoodies. I admit we weren't planning to go to church. The day after Christmas, we had hit the King of Prussia Mall. When the shoe salesman went to measure Max for his fancy black loafers, Max said, "I need new shoes because my daddy died."

Your child speaks the facts, but you cannot fall apart in Stride Rite.

"His daddy's plane crashed on the twenty-second," I said.

The shoe salesman looked at me with confusion and compassion. I'm sure that, if he could have, he would have given Max a free pair of loafers and mini-Brian-Gold-Toe-socks.

※

On December 30 in Baltimore and on January 4 in Huntington Beach, everyone was a mess. People told me I was amazingly strong that week, and I was, in part because it was moving for me to witness so many people showing up to honor the man I loved. We were all heartbroken. With a youthful out-of-order death comes the great wake-up call: *It could have been me, my brother, my son, or my husband.*

In the eulogies I wrote for Brian, I spoke directly to the fact that we live on borrowed time. I wasn't subtle, because this truth is urgent.

The song we closed Brian's second life ceremony with was one that came to me on the flight from Maryland to California: In "Live Like We're Dying," Kris Allen sings: "We only got 86,400 seconds in a day."

Brian knew that time was borrowed and that time flies.

One minute into the song, Allen sings: "And, if your plane fell out of the skies/Who would you call with your last goodbye?"

Chapter Eleven

In the last videos taken of Brian, he is with our kids, my brother, and my brother's boys—Patrick, Danny, and John—launching model rockets on the beach. It was Thanksgiving 2011, a few weeks before the plane crash.

Rocketry as a hobby took off in the decades following the Soviet Union's mid-20th-century launch of Sputnik I. Children in the United States and Canada—Brian being one of the latter—began making and firing off rockets at home in earnest, causing more backyard explosions and finger amputations than ever. Experimenting with rocket science, young Brian and his father set a barn door on fire; Brian's father almost lost an ear.

At Christmas 2011, after Brian's fall to earth caused a major rupture in the flow and order of our good life, it hit me how especially fortunate we had been in our last weeks together. How grateful I was that we had given thanks over a bountiful Thanksgiving meal with extended family. The beach in Mexico was our special retreat, a dream rest-and-relaxation spot that Brian and I had made real and regular. The last time we'd had all the McGuires together in Mexico—grandparents, aunts, uncles, and cousins—I had been pregnant with Mel. In 2011, she was eight.

Brian turned into a kid on that beach. He turned into a kid

around model rockets and fire. He was a pyromaniac. In Mexico, he and I would build massive pyres in the fire pit in front of our house. We knew it wasn't the safest thing to do, but it was fun. One time, we constructed a towering tent of driftwood and fallen palm fronds. Brian walked backward away from the pile, drawing a line of gas in the sand. He told everyone to stand back and lit a match—woohoo—a low flame ripped up the beach and blew fiery palm fronds everywhere. Luckily, nobody was hurt.

Another time, one New Year's Eve, he came up to the house after stoking a beach fire and his eyebrows were gone. The front of his hairline was singed. He'd already started going bald, so he decided to ring in the New Year with his head completely shaven. He kept that look until the day he died, not because of the sexy factor, but because maintaining a hairless head was super efficient.

Apart from his brain, which was advanced-high-tech caliber—and, lack of hair aside—we used to joke that Brian was not too far removed physically from our early ancestors. Standing compact and buff, he was half caveman. He loved red meat and salt—the first preservative. When we joked about having him taxidermized, he said he'd like to spend part of his time in a corner of our house, keeping an eye on us.

"That's creepy!" I said. "I'd put you in the zoo, in that evolution exhibit. I'd set you between the caveman and modern-day man."

We laughed: He really did fit in the middle.

Of course, we couldn't taxidermy Brian, but we did have him cremated—as he wished. There is definitely finality in fire.

The December of his death, Brian was traveling more than usual for business. The U.S. solar industry was experiencing a rough patch. But still, he had made it to all our kids' holiday shows even though Max was in one show one day, the girls were in another show the next day, and Brian had a board meeting in Nevada scheduled in between. I'd wanted to call and tell him not to stress too much to come, it wouldn't be the last time the kids would be in a play, but I knew he would come anyway.

I can't remember everything about those performances, but Max sang the *Golden Girls* theme song, "Thank You for Being a Friend," and Melanie played a seed in a skit.

"I remember all the seeds were going somewhere," she would tell me years later. "And I was the one with the longest journey."

※

Patrick, Danny, and John were sixteen, fourteen, and twelve, respectively, when they lost their uncle. All of them came to the funeral home, but only Patrick made it to the Celebration of Life. The boys were old enough to understand their loss, yet probably not quite old enough to deal with the painful emotions surrounding it. Naturally, nobody asked them to do anything they weren't ready to do.

Brian's sister, Julie, had three kids. She and Brian had always been very tight, and we vacationed together every summer in Canada. Julie's youngest two could not understand their loss—Lotus was only three, and Tao two. Seven-year-old Emma was attached to Mel and Brooke, though, and Brian had been like a father figure to her before Julie got married. Emma was there on December 30 to touch her uncle in his casket.

Within days of Brian's passing, Emma said, "I want a new daddy for Brookie!" We were all taken aback. Emma was so young, but she saw her favorite cousin aching. It occurred to her that if Brooke could lose her daddy overnight, the same could happen to hers. What if?

Kids speak their truth, whether it is comfortable or not. "Fixing" the family is at the top of their minds, even if adults can't fathom such a fix. As close as she had been to Brian and to us as a couple, Julie always made it clear that she would care for Melanie, Brooke, and Max as if they were her own, and she has, whenever I have needed her to. She said then and there, too, after Emma spoke so soon after Brian's death, "We don't want you ever to think that we don't want you to meet someone."

Until you walk in another person's shoes—specifically, until you experience the trauma of someone you love dying—it can be easy to talk about what to say and do and what not to say and do regarding death, grief, and those who are grieving. But boy, is it complicated. Most people, including me, don't know what to say to the heartbroken. Feeling guilty, we say nothing, or we say things we later regret. I've learned, though, that compassion and forgiveness go both ways when humans struggle in the dark together.

When Max told the shoe salesman straight out that he needed new shoes because his daddy had died, I managed not to fall apart.

In the first few hours and days, though, I cried uncontrollably in front of everyone in the house, including the kids. Or I hid my sobs under the stream of the shower.

Navigating feelings, spirituality, conversations, and relationships through mourning, open caskets, and the gaping holes the dead leave behind can be horrible and scary; but it somehow always bears repeating—empathy in such times is key. Acceptance is crucial. Step softly into those other shoes. What one child can handle, another cannot. What one adult can do, another cannot. I plowed through many tasks in robot mode, or, summoning Brian's efficiency, in Brian mode, and that was okay; but, though it may sound contradictory, I knew I also had to allow myself to be in fully raw, messy, and flailing human being mode. To help my kids, I had to be real, everything, and present.

I needed to learn what to do for them, how to help them, and how not to screw up—all while suddenly having become a blank slate. It wasn't just the rug that had been pulled out from under me, it was my entire world. I was missing my key supporter, my key sounding board. Off-balance, I would need time to figure out what came after "I am," because I would no longer be able to say, "I am Eileen Robertson, Brian Robertson's wife; I am Mrs. Robertson." The words "Mrs." and "wife" changed meaning for me after Brian died. I could still be his best friend and partner—I would be—but that was it. No wife, no Mrs.

"I am a mother," I told myself. "The past and the future are way too painful to think about, so focus on the present. Focus on *I am; I am a mother.* Breathe and sit with wonder."

Brian's death and the loss of my central identity forced me to become less Eileen-centric, less E- and me-centric. It was me and the kids, not against the world now, but fully nestling into the kindness of the world.

As the mother of Melanie, Brooke, and Max, I decided to spend conscious, one-on-one time with each of our children and to check in on them often. Together, we were going to be okay. We were lucky to have each other and to be traveling this unplanned detour together.

Starting the night of Brian's death, at my parents' home, the kids and I instinctively began to cocoon. We would continue this cocooning for the next six months in our Huntington Beach home, until the school year ended. We pulled two mattresses into the master bedroom, set them beside the California King bed Brian and I had shared, and rotated bodies—one kid slept with me every night, two slept on the floor. Every night, I read children's books aloud: *Buddha at Bedtime, Peaceful Piggy Meditation*, and *I Think, I Am!*

I wouldn't do everything right. In my comfortable lucky life, I had allowed the extraordinary to become ordinary—something my father had always warned me against. I had slacked some on parenting, especially with Melanie, my mini-me, the one who would push my buttons until I'd shout: "Brian, help me out here—deal with your daughter! Calgon, take me away!"

So many times, I relied on him to be the better parent to our older daughter. Most parents admit parenting is sometimes a tag-team deal: "You've got it this time, honey. Please."

But I passed the buck a lot when it came to Mel, and we did not have the best relationship when Brian died. For all I know, when she lost her father she might have been thinking, "Now what? I'm left with *you*?"

After Brian died, Mel and I entered into a truce.

I had work to do to repair our relationship. I didn't exactly know how, but I did know to start with a huge apology for my over-the-top reactions when she didn't unload the dishwasher or pick up a pile of clothes. Push my Irish edge and I'm on fire—see, I still make excuses for being the zero-to-sixty Scary Mommy. But in the cocoon, I finally said, "Mel, I am so sorry I haven't been patient with you."

I needed all the kids' forgiveness, and I asked for it then, in the cocoon.

The forgiveness each of us offered each other opened us up to a level of connection we had not yet experienced.

A week after Brian died, I went on a long walk with Brooke. She was seven, and looking at the little grasses coming up between the sidewalk cracks she said to me, "When I was little, I used to notice all the details and now I don't notice as much anymore."

How was it that messages seemingly intended for me were coming from every direction?

In the terrible haze since Brian's death—and prior to it—what details had I been rushing past and missing? If I was going to train to become a yoga teacher—and I was—I'd have to slow down and take notice, like young children and ancient spiritual masters do. My roles in business and entrepreneurship had taken me far, as had the roles of wife and mother, but in all the strategizing, organizing, and doing, I had put matters of the spirit on the back burner. Seeing Brian's body had been the starkest reminder that we are so much more than our overachieving minds and bodies.

Brian's death placed spirit in front of us all.

And Max. Young Max, who would have his table-throwing tantrum at school and test me by screaming that he hated me, also had his calmer moments processing Brian's death.

After we returned to Huntington Beach, about a week after Brian died, Max said, "I figured it out. We can put the spirit back in Daddy."

When I told him that was impossible because we had cremated him, he said, "What's that?"

"It means we burned Daddy in a fire."

"What?! You burned Daddy? I don't want to live anymore!"

Holy shit, I thought. What am I saying? What am I doing? I don't know how to do this.

"I want to live on Mars!" Max shouted, tears streaming down his face.

I understood this was Max's way of expressing that he didn't want to live feeling the way he was feeling. Life on Earth with no Daddy was way too much—and way too little—for him.

"Mars is not available," I told him. I was now crying too. "I'm sorry."

We talked about how much Brian loved fire and agreed that cremation was what he would have wanted.

"Okay," Max said. "So you're going to get me a new dad, and

I want him to be just like Daddy. Just make sure he's not a midget."

I started laughing.

"Mommy, why are you laughing?"

"What makes you think I'm going to marry a midget?" I said.

"I saw a mean one in *Elf*, and I don't·want one like that."

I caught my breath. The term "midget" wasn't an appropriate word, and I would one day explain that—and Will Ferrell humor—to Max.

For the time being, I just said, "Well, I'm not ready to get you a new daddy yet, and you don't have to worry because there are lots of people who will help fill Daddy's shoes. When I am ready, I promise—no midgets."

Being ready to find Max a new dad? Nothing could have been farther from my mind, or closer to Max's. From that day forward, he was on a mission.

At the airport, a few months after Brian's death, Max noticed a father traveling with two little kids. The man was covered in tattoos and looked like a rock star.

Max tapped me on the arm. "I want one like that one," he said.

Time would need to pass for Max to get what he wanted, and in getting what he wanted, new challenges would arise.

Chapter Twelve

Watching the kids grieve felt like watching dominoes fall. There was a strange choreography to their tumbling. Each of them felt sad or bad, but not necessarily all at once. The weight of Brian's death was heavy, but it was not the same degree of heaviness at the same time. The kids also seemed tuned in—among themselves—regarding me. I can't be sure, but it seemed that, if they sensed I was in a better than usual space one day, one of the three of them could let their grief loose. One would simply be "in a mood" for a spell, or would rage with all their might, or would cry.

Max's processing of Brian's death was the most immediate and visceral. He told me he wanted to kill himself when I denied him ice cream. With three young children, I didn't have time to read books this time around, as I had after my sister died. I directly sought out real, live experts on children's grief.

Debbie delaCuesta was another one of my down-to-earth angels. I went seeking guidance for Max, but her first question whenever we walked through her office door was always directed at me: "How are *you* doing?"

Like a flight attendant, she knew I couldn't help my kids unless I was breathing. Was my oxygen mask secured and functioning? Okay, then. We could proceed.

With Debbie, I learned much more than I thought I knew about the importance of modeling for our children. She helped me forgive my Scary Mommy moments by confirming that I would screw up at times. I did screw up, still do, always will. Much to my horror, as the kids have grown and made their own less than stellar choices, I've used the awful line: "Your Dad would be so disappointed."

Really, Eileen?

With Debbie, I learned that modeling sadness was not only fine, it was encouraged. I still cried to myself and by myself, but I also told the kids, "I'm really sad. I'm really missing Daddy right now."

We talked about Brian all the time; we kept his name and spirit alive.

For the most part, Brooke—always the one to care for everyone else first—hid her pain from me. She tried holding it all together during the six months we lived in California immediately following Brian's death. School support was huge for the girls, but I did have to pick Brooke up once midday because she had gone to the school nurse complaining of not feeling well. I asked, "Is it your stomach? Is it something you ate?" and she said, "Maybe."

It took her several minutes before she began crying and told me that she had heard an airplane flying over the school and had been thinking about Daddy in his final moments. She was worried sick that he had been scared.

"He thought he was going to get out," I told her. "He was only scared in the very last second. One second."

Things would get worse for Brooke after we left California and moved to Maryland. Melanie, my stoic mini-me, tried, and succeeded, for a long time to emulate my real and supposed strength. But she would unleash a mega-wave of grief in Maryland, too, telling me, "I had a bad dream. Daddy was there, and I made him a gift but forgot to give it to him. When I went to give it to him, I couldn't find him, because he was dead."

What could I say other than "I'm sorry?"

Each of my children was waking and walking in foreign territory.

One night, while I was snuggling with Max and reading him to sleep, he said, "You know, Mommy, I found Daddy. He's in the underground world. I go there sometimes and talk to him."

I wondered if Max's underground world was a silver-clouded plain as the Irish imagined it. Did Max and his father build bonfires and castles there?

※

When it came to finding support for my kids, I was incredibly picky. This had been true since the moment I found out I was pregnant with Mel and began devouring books on parenting. I'd curated a mini-library. *The Parent's Tao Te Ching* was my go-to resource. By the time Max was in utero my "parenting section" contained books on children's developmental stages and learning, discipline and play, nutrition and sleep.

Intent on seeking knowledge on how to raise our kids, Brian

and I were drawn to Maria Montessori and her methods. The Montessori philosophy that children are not "little adults" rang true to us, and we went all in.

There are countless statistics on issues grieving children experience in school—lower grades, poorer attendance, difficulty concentrating in class, and so on. While it's true that each of my kids would have their challenging moments following Brian's death, for the most part, school was life support—for them and for me. Montessori teachers and staff made sure the classroom continued to be a place of routine, challenge, compassion, and comfort.

Classmates wrote condolence cards, and each Robertson child was encouraged to ask for extra help, or quiet time, or talk time with the school counselor if necessary. Because I was so far from my parents and siblings, my yoga and wellness peers, parents of the kids' friends, and groups like the YMCA Indian Princess dads became my extended family. At every sport and community event, the kids and I felt embraced and empowered.

The first Father's Day without Brian, Dave and Donna visited. Who could possibly fill Brian's shoes better at the girls' father-daughter dances than his own father? The schools presented each of our kids with a photo collage of past Father's Day events. There was Max in Brian's arms, giving him a gift. There was Brooke in Brian's arms, giving him a gift. There was Mel in Brian's arms, giving him a gift. They still have these collages in their bedrooms today. The Indian Princess fathers also paid tribute to Brian by gifting the kids with photos and mementos. Father's Day would always be bittersweet for the kids. Mother's Day, I discovered, would be harder on me. The man who had made me a mother was gone.

For those first six months—the last we would live in California—the girls especially took to relying on each other. I would learn from Debbie, from teachers, and from other widows that this was their way of protecting me, of keeping me from grieving more than I already was. Who knows if my showing up that day for Brooke and telling her that Brian was only scared in his last second of life comforted her at all, but I showed up. I listened and talked things through with her as best and as truthfully as I could. Then I took her home.

The scrambling to be what children need most when a parent dies cannot be predicted or dictated. Additional support and a conscious effort toward small and great acts of kindness are crucial. I stayed as clear-headed and open-hearted as I could for Melanie, Brooke, and Max, but without our friends and teachers I am sure I would not have been enough.

❋

My intention to stay busy and involved in the business that focused on corporate wellbeing was derailed, in part, by Max's troubles as a suddenly fatherless four-year-old child. Had nobody known about the loss he was suffering, had they only seen him kicking his teacher and screaming in the school hallway that he was going to run home, get his dad's hunting gun (which was never kept in the house), and shoot everyone, I can certainly imagine what conclusions they might have drawn. Children can only reason and process so much at that age, and, though we've all been told "You never know what someone is struggling with, so err on the side of kindness," we do forget. We judge.

Our California community did not forget to err on the side of kindness. At school, teachers led special discussions and lessons revolving around the death of a parent, because kids are wise and inquisitive, and they fear that if a classmate's Daddy can die suddenly, so might theirs.

✳

Melanie, Brooke, and Max teach me, to this day, how grief moves. In talking all these years later about the song the kids sang at the service in Huntington Beach, Mel remembers, "I grabbed my guitar because it was the only thing I could put a finger on."

Max realized at age ten that, although he loves Mike, he doesn't want to call him "Dad" anymore. He does not have access to his biological father and never will. Years later, Max still asks for details: Was there a parachute? Why not? Why us? Why not somebody else?

I listen. And I answer with my own version of "I don't know."

So many people have held space for my children as they explore and reconcile the paradoxes of life and death and the unknowing. I mentioned that with my grief, decades after the loss of my sister and with three kids in tow, I didn't have time to read books on children's grief or wade through research. Some of the statistics I have heard make me shake my head anyway. For instance, on their tenth anniversary of Children's Grief Awareness Day fact sheet, Highmark Caring Place cited the following findings from a 2009 Comfort Zone Camp Childhood Bereavement Study: "56% of respondents who lost a parent growing up would trade a year of their life for one day more with their departed parent," and "72% believe their life would have been 'much better' if their parent hadn't died so young."

I would never disparage those who dedicate their lives to helping young people wade through loss, but findings such as these reiterate for me the fact that there is more work to be done regarding how we help children who are grieving. There is so much we *do not* and *cannot* know, but why highlight what's missing instead of focusing on what is possible again? My kids and I carried enough sadness on our own; we needed no help in feeling worse by dwelling on impossible tradeoffs and what-ifs. When I became a widow, I sought positive influences in other widows, friends, angels, and guides—I modeled this for my kids as best I could.

Still, I recognize that grief is a journey only the individual can take. Support and modeling are crucial, but what works for me will not necessarily work for anyone else, my own flesh and blood included.

At the memorial service in Baltimore, Brooke was seen sitting alone outside on a concrete block. She was in lotus position, her back straight as a ruler, her eyes closed. Her hands were resting palms-up on her knees in *shuni mudra*, which unites fire and connection and helps provide stability. Brooke had witnessed me on my mat, she had joined me there more than once; and there she was now, sitting with whatever version of spirit she had thus far come to know. She was feeling things she did not know and was trying to sit with them in grace.

I sometimes want desperately to solve my children's puzzles, to help them put the pieces together so they form a coherent and meaningful picture. What could I say, I wonder, from my adult experiences and deep work on transformation, to help keep them from any further or unnecessary suffering? I don't know, because, from what I do know, this is not how the world works. I tell our children, "All we have been through only makes us stronger." I think of telling them that I'm grateful for this journey, and that they need to come to this gratefulness—*or not*—for themselves. But what I tell them may make no difference. They are exploring and discovering and coming to answers, not entirely by themselves, but for themselves.

Chapter Thirteen

W. H. Auden was twenty-one years gone when his poem "Stop all the clocks" gained a new audience in the movie *Four Weddings and a Funeral*. In the poem, he writes about longing, after the death of a loved one, to pause time and hush sound, namely music and a barking dog. He mentions, as well, the moon, sun, and stars, the woods and water, saying, in effect, "trash it all."

> Let aeroplanes circle moaning overhead
> Scribbling on the sky the message He Is Dead . . .

I was never one to turn to poems for solace or direction, but I relate to the desire to halt time and reduce the daily static after someone dies. In the California cocoon the kids and I inhabited from January through June 2012, we lived semi-subdued in a temporary and suspended time zone. We controlled what felt like a foreign space by somehow resisting acknowledgment of what it no longer was for us. We were not exactly in shock, we weren't zombies, but we lived in the Huntington Beach house while parts of it felt dead.

The master bedroom was our domain, and this is where we wrapped ourselves in Brian's clothes, talked and cried, wondered and slept. Over the course of those six months, sometimes I didn't know which was worse: Tucking in together after another sunset without our fearless leader or waking up with another sunrise to realize there was no way to beam him back.

There is no going back. There are 86,400 seconds in each day, those seconds roll on, and before you know it, it's the one-month anniversary of your beloved's death. It is the first Mother's Day, and then the first Father's Day. It is the first end-of-the-school-year performances he won't show up for.

In the song "Live Like We're Dying," Kris Allen reminds us that we can do our best to love the seconds we are given, or we can throw them all away. If I could toss the darkest hours that circumstances have forced me to plod through, I wouldn't, because, as clichéd as it sounds, those surreal hours got me to where I am today.

I'm no physicist, but I have learned that time is relative—it can move forward at warp speed and as slow as molasses, simultaneously. Some of the sharpest, most innovative minds have promoted theories about parallel universes where time moves differently, and, while I hold no expectation of even Brian's MIT peers making any of these miraculous mirrored spaces accessible any time soon, physicists and poets are on to something, and I'm listening. Auden's opening command in "Stop all the clocks," where he references the awful nature of clocks to simply go on doing what they are built to do despite tragedy blowing a minute wide open, rings true for me.

That poem is great, except for the closing line: "For nothing now can ever come to any good."

To me, that's bullshit.

Did I ever feel, at any point in my life, that "nothing now can ever come to any good?" No. At times I've felt lost, caged, or gutted, but nobody would ever call me a pessimist or a Debbie Downer. I know despair but cannot dwell there. I won't dwell there. The truth is I can't bear to sink into the couch in misery. When the darkness comes for me, I sit with it and acknowledge it. To lie around moping, letting it blanket me, goes against every fiber of my being.

If I had wanted to go fetal when the kids and I returned to California, there were dozens of people who wouldn't have allowed it. In a chain reaction of love, my brother Jimmy's wife, Gina, offered to take care of their kids so that Jimmy could accompany me, Melanie, Brooke, and Max on our flight back to the West Coast. For days, my brother sat with me in Brian's home office, shuffling through files, figuring out passwords, deciphering legalese, and getting the necessary papers in line to deal with the estate. Brian and I had lawyers, wills, and matters concerning our estate in order, but it wasn't *orderly*. It wasn't organized in neat boxes, filed, labeled, and stamped. The process, after Jimmy left, would prove to be achingly slow. Legal matters drive home the fundamental truth that it takes time to let go.

My brother, fulfilling his role as big brother, saved me. My parents being with us in California for the first four weeks of 2012 saved us, too. After my family left, the number of friends who continued to carry on with support was astounding.

The first Christmas party Brian and I held in 2009, at our new Huntington Beach home, we invited everyone we knew. Twenty-five people attended. At Christmas 2011, we had over 150 party guests, and this was after we had gracefully figured out how not to invite everyone we wished we could. All these people, though, whether they had attended our final family Christmas party or not, were at our door when the kids and I returned from the East Coast, wondering what they could do to help.

When it came to food, I didn't have to cook a thing but scrambled eggs for months. My girlfriends created a *Genius* sign-up for people to bring us meals, and they were so good at managing this service that we never ate spaghetti, ziti, and lasagna all in one week.

Without asking, by simply opening my eyes and looking around, I found that everyone I needed was there—they had always been there. When I had used up all my energy trying to be Mom and Dad to the kids, Brynn, our babysitter at the time, took over. Missy, the mother of Brooke's best friend in kindergarten and also my very good friend, just happened to know a lot about aircraft manufacturing because of the company she ran. She was a key to helping me understand what happened to Brian. There are earth-bound angels, and they provide a loving, giving, timeless, and mystical power.

✳

"We do not know/if there be fairies now/Or no," Auden writes in his poem "Belief."

I believe in fairies, guardian angels, and supportive spirits, and at the same time, I'm thankful for Auden, scientists, poets, anyone, for admitting that we do not know it all, we are still seeking. The struggle is timeless and real; it applies to everything. With hindsight, I can see that Brian's death and its aftermath were like a crucible— or composed of a series of crucible moments—but, when the kids and I returned to California after his death, though I knew life would go on, I had no idea what it would look like.

I did know, though I didn't admit it to many people, that I was growing from the experience of losing Brian. Through the most hellish days, I could feel my growth—in fact, acknowledging it kept me alive. Transformation is a gift, even when it is a gift we think we do not want and even when it means all the plans we made are suddenly impossible.

Having no structure—no familiar handholds—restricted me, kept me from knowing all I wanted to know, but rarely did I lose awareness of having and making choices. Choice and alternate stories exist in every small shift we make and in each step we take with pain, despite pain, regardless of how unaware we are in the moment that *this . . . is . . . progress.*

The kids and I could progress because we had the support of our community. The more people stepped in to buoy the kids, the more I felt like I had some freedom and space to practice self-care. I reached out to Debbie delaCuesta originally to ask for help with Max, but Debbie became one of my most illuminating guides. When she first asked me how I was doing, I responded with a somewhat embarrassed, "I feel like I am having some sort of a spiritual awakening." The synchronicities following Brian's crash were too many and too precise to be chalked up to coincidence. "I get that we are most certainly spirits living a human experience," I said to Debbie. "But what is really going on?"

Debbie was not only a licensed family therapist, she was also a spiritual-growth coach. She introduced me to experiments of the psyche to which I had never been exposed. Some resonated, and some did not. She referred me to two shamans. Prior to meeting either one, the only thing I knew about shamans was that they were said to be gifted in seeing beyond the veil. Jim Morrison of the Doors dabbled in shamanism. My school girlfriends and I had posters of him on our walls; he was the closest illustration of "trippy" we had.

The first shaman I visited played drums and told me my spirit guide animals were a trio of horses. Maybe one day I'll explore that. Michael, the second shaman, would be the one to say something really unexpected, and in retrospect, profound.

Leaving the cocoon of our house in Huntington Beach and driving through the gate of a cookie-cutter community in Orange County in my soccer mom minivan, I had my doubts. Suburbia—was this the typical dwelling space of a shaman? When I rang the doorbell, a completely non-trippy woman greeted me, and then led me to a home office straight out of Anywhere, U.S.A. She offered me tea, told me that Michael had trained and worked with Don Miguel Ruiz, author of *The Four Agreements*, and asked me to take a seat at a small table covered with several huge crystals.

Michael entered the room and after some small talk, we began our session. I was asked to choose one of the crystals on the table, and he chose one as well. He asked me to focus on our choices and to close my eyes. Once the question *WTF am I doing in Orange County holding this stone?* whizzed through my consciousness, I stilled. I did as I was directed and then was guided through a meditation. I was going with the flow, but what came next I was not expecting.

"Brian, you, and a third person," he began. "A man you will meet about eighteen months after Brian's passing—made an agreement before you were born. The three of you made a pact, agreeing that you will work together on this earthly plane, toward a shared purpose. Everything is unfolding as the three of you planned, and when you meet this third person, who is coming, you will know. You will not question. He will pick up where Brian left off."

Michael then gently guided me out of the meditative session, but I didn't know whether to cry or to bolt. He apologized for telling me what he had sensed or seen, saying, "I hope that's not too much."

OMG. How can what he said feel so true?

I had been feeling as if Brian's death, and now the kids and I in the cocoon, was unfolding as if it had all been planned. I wasn't upset, but I had absolutely no idea what I would do, should do, or could do with what this shaman said. There was nothing to do but wait and see.

※

One thing, I realized quickly, that I could not do (because it served no one and was a waste of time) was to argue with reality. Our loss hurt. Darkness is as much a part of life as light. Darkness is there, and we have the capacity to let it in like an old friend, be with it, and then turn it gently around and release it as the creative and regenerative force it can be.

The transformation of pain and the self is not a burning or turning away—the goal is not to deny or destroy our sadness or our past. We cannot grow only by leaning into joy. Transformation begins with a spark of faith that allows us to lean into the hurt, turning it first to flame and eventually to fire. It's not easy; at times it feels impossibly hard. But we fuel and increase our own light each time we make it through hell and back. Transformation is a turning after a turning after a turning; and the energy generated in the process inspires, incubates, and attracts whatever, or whoever, is meant to come next.

I'm a McGuire, but I didn't learn until my trip to Ireland with Mary Kay that Halloween is derived from the Celtic festival of Samhain. Samhain, held on October 31, and Bealtaine, held on May Day, ring in, respectively, winter and summer. My Irish ancestors believed that during Samhain, boundaries between the world as we know it and the spirit world break down. During these liminal periods, where the balance between the dark and the light shifts, we can communicate easier with the dead. Stories-high bonfires lit during Samhain and Bealtaine usher in death and rebirth.

When the kids and I were in full cocoon mode in California, whenever I sensed I was standing too long in the shadows, I forced myself to remember that the kids had lost their sun, and now had only their moon. In the darkness, their gaze was on me. An entire universe was buoying us, but, in terms of parenting, I was *it*. I was the one to stay alive, to protect and guide them, to know what to do. In the very unsettling state of "I have no idea what comes next," I had to balance our time tucked in and healing versus getting back out in the world.

Our cocoon was our balm and salvation, our reenergizing center. During the day, the kids went to school, and I kept myself busy. The four of us ventured, like young toddlers learning to walk, away from and back to our primary source of warmth and security. We functioned in the spaces that made life bearable and in the clubs we never wanted to belong to (widows' clubs and grieving children's clubs). But, to build our stamina and bravery back up again, we had to spend time together in the darkness—unsteady and unsure, newly unformed and slowly transforming—until we were healed—enough—and ready to rise into full flight toward new light.

＊

Although I didn't know it, meeting Brian for the first time was a life-altering moment. In turning toward the possibility of us, I was trusting my gut, trusting the universe, and entering the unknown. I chose to take a chance on a guy who did not fit my plan, but who turned out to be perfect for me. Brian was the man who would radically alter the trajectory I believed I was on—more than once.

When he and I chose to get married, we thought we knew. There was science at play in chemistry, in pheromones, and practicality was part of our decision. We both valued family, hard work, traveling the world and making a difference in it. Trusting in the universe and the good juju of fairies and angels on our side, we knew. We fell in love, we called each other soul mates, and we took a leap and bound it with the fantasy of "forever."

If we only really knew.

I'd had this partner for over a decade, and now here I was struggling with uncomfortable questions: Would I be single forever? Is it wrong that I want to be single forever? How could I ever be as lucky again? These questions fell on top of more practical but equally hard questions. I had known since Brian's first Ceremony of Life in Baltimore that we would move back east to be closer to family, but making decisions related to that move wasn't easy. It was all on me. There was no more dividing and conquering of tasks. Brian was not there to ask me, "Have you thought of—?" or to say, "Good job!"

But again, when I looked around, everyone I needed was right there. I knew that the universe and our communities—west and east—had our backs. I trusted that the future would look like whatever it was going to look like if I kept breathing, moving, choosing whatever sliver of the silver lining I could find. Our life-altering experiences, amazing or devastating, illuminate life's multi-dimensionality: Life is a series of good, innocent, ridiculous, profound, compassionate, and painful moments combined and set apart in light of one another—in juxtaposition. Life is never out to get us or unfair or perfect or too good to be true.

If we could figure out how to bottle life's attitude toward life— life just is. Being present is the most liminal and promising state we can achieve. We might learn to be okay with softening our grip, yielding, and letting go. Teetering on the threshold of our old ways and our possible new ways 24/7 is impossible, untenable, but, in threshold moments and places, all potential exists.

When pain is dumped on us suddenly, we meet hell, and it's a beast. The last thing we can think of is potential, or a new life, or the way out. Many of the paths we try are dead ends. But the road out of hell is straighter than we think. The key is to move forward by accepting, forgiving, or loving what we can't face. The map isn't hard to decipher, but I won't say it is easy to turn in the right direction. Pain has a funny way of keeping us lost.

The cocoon we build with others is necessary and nourishing, but it's only a temporary buffer. When I close my eyes and picture the bedroom in California where the kids and I all slept together for six months, I see the bed, the white sheets, a cocoon. I see us kicking, tossing, and shapeshifting before settling and coming to rest beneath those sheets.

As for feeling secure, Max told me early on that, if I didn't find a new dad quick, I had better buy a gun. Knowing I didn't trust myself to ever point a gun in the right direction, I made sure to set the alarm on the house every night. There was no way I could have forgotten this task anyway, because Max would incessantly remind me to batten down the hatches before bed.

During this cocooning phase, though their sense of security had been rocked, the kids stopped fighting—the universe had called for a ceasefire. Together, we were warm. Together, we took longer and deeper breaths as the weeks marched toward spring. Come summer-time, we would be up in the air, suspended in yet one more temporary liminal space between past and future, flying east into the sunrise like tentative but agile butterflies.

CHAPTER FOURTEEN

While doing my yoga teacher training, I worked my way through a sun salutation, and then sat with my eyes closed, in savasana. When I opened my eyes and looked into the mirror, because of where the two large mirror panels met, my image was split in two. I laughed. I had been working so hard at filling my role as mother and as father, moon and sun, yin and yang, and there I was.

So many people had stepped in as surrogate mothers and fathers for the kids, stepped out of their comfort zones, talked to me daily while I was in cocoon mode. My sister was my best friend. My yoga friends and I cried on our mats. Friends made cross-country trips to visit and to make sure I wasn't drowning. My best friends were with me when I tried to enjoy my first glass of wine since the plane crash, and they included me and the kids in their Friday and Saturday night plans.

Masculine energy and Brian-energy was showing up for the kids, and I was grateful. Melanie and Brooke's soccer coach, who had daughters their same ages, took extra care to make sure my girls were okay on the field without Daddy on the sidelines. The Kaw Tribe of the Orange County Indian Princesses, which was the key community outside the home for Brian's relationship with Melanie and Brooke, went above and beyond to continue to include the girls in all their activities. Brian had joined the tribe when we first moved to California, and he and the girls loved earning badges for their vests, participating in the pinewood derby races and camping on the beach and in the mountains. They never missed a single father-daughter dance. Melanie and Brooke had created strong bonds with the other father-daughter couples in their tribes.

Before graduating out of the tribe, usually in fourth or fifth grade, Indian Princesses have the opportunity to earn the most special badge—the California Bear Badge. This entails a project you work on with your father, and it's a big deal. How were the girls going to have this experience without Brian? The Kaw dads figured it out and supported them the whole way through. Right before we left California, I was invited to break protocol and attend the badge-earning ceremony as a mom. During the ceremony, Mel and Brooke presented scrapbooks they had each put together, highlighting their most precious Kaw father-daughter memories. I have never seen so many fathers lose it in one room.

My heart broke knowing that Max would never make the same memories with his father as the girls had. Before the crash, Brian and Max had joined the father-son version of the Indian Princesses, the Indian Guides. Their first camping trip was scheduled the following year, after Max would have turned five.

Dan, one of the Kaw dads with a son the same age as Max, generously offered to take Max with him and his son that next year on the camping trip. Max was so brave and so desperate to experience what the girls had that we returned west after moving to Maryland to give him this gift. He experienced his first father-son camping trip with a group of amazing surrogate fathers.

Next-door neighbors and Brian's work colleagues were there for us. In 2011, Melanie had been into studying electricity and had chosen to play Thomas Edison at the Montessori School's Historical Halloween show. Brian and I had bought her a bunch of books on electricity and would find her staying up way past bedtime, secretly reading these books with a flashlight.

After Brian died, Mel came up with the idea to make a solar energy–powered go-cart. I was pretty good at figuring things out, but there was no way I'd be able to help her with that dream. I called one of Brian's engineer colleagues, Adam, and asked if he would mind meeting with Melanie to help. He was thrilled to be asked and they worked on the vehicle until it was fully functional. It cost twice what they had budgeted and drove much faster than anything an eight-year-old should be driving, but Mel had a blast. She felt connected to her father every time she worked on that project.

* ·

Six summers after the kids and I left California, a female orca whale named Tahlequah swam in the waters between Washington state and B.C., Canada, carrying her dead calf's carcass. The mother whale pushed her little one, who had only been alive in this world for thirty minutes, through the Salish Sea for an "unprecedented" period of time—almost three weeks. Falling behind her pod,

Tahlequah risked her own survival. The world watched, mourning her loss and our role in it. Thousands of people wrote poems and letters to the *Seattle Times*, renewing their vows to do more to save endangered species, touching on mother/daughter bonds, or sharing experiences of grieving for a child lost to suicide or a child stillborn.

This mother whale's grieving was seen as mystical, mythical, primal. Hundreds of thousands of people around the globe tuned in to bear witness to this otherworldly and yet familiar narrative, where an animal did not want to let go, where an animal carried a body until that body began to turn into what it was born into—salt and water—two of the components of human tears.

For a while, via drone footage, humans became attuned to a holding-on that was beyond wondrous. We then surrendered our sorrow to the reality that the baby never stood a chance, and we hoped for its mother to let go and to remain among the living.

I am lucky: I've had a lot of practice accepting what is and have learned that looking back and dwelling on what could have been doesn't work. I live without regret, partly because my Catholicism taught me to forgive myself and others. The sacrament of reconciliation gives us an opportunity to start again—and again—with a clean slate. This is not to say I don't do things that aren't regrettable. We all do. But there is no power in regretting what's been done, because we already did it! Regret is a dead end, a stuck emotion. Regret will keep us spinning in circles longer than an overzealous spin class instructor will.

Holding on—to regrets, to people, or to things—can be

limiting, exhausting, and sometimes life-threatening.

Tahlequah the orca, in pushing and diving to retrieve her dead baby for so many days, missed foraging opportunities. Trailing her pod increased her risk of being hit by boaters. Even with other members of her community assisting her in her mission to keep her baby afloat and possibly feeding her, the added stress on her and on any of these already stressed animals could have proved fatal. Orcas are apex predators—but they are struggling to adapt to environmental changes. They have to keep on swimming in order to survive.

When I stood at Brian's casket at Al Khuner's funeral home, I was able to let go of him, to accept his death immediately. The vivid impact of his energy being gone was all it took. His deadness was so final. But it did take me a while to recognize that I was attached—to Brian, to ideas, to things, and to dreams. Leave it to my sister to bring me to a realization I had not yet achieved in all my years of yoga or transformational workshops. I had been living as if Brian were mine.

A few weeks after he died, Mary Kay called to tell me she had gotten a sign. We both believe in signs, having received so many from Tricia, over so many decades.

"I'd forgotten about wanting to learn this Dave Matthews song," she said.

Mary Kay is a guitar player, and long before Brian's crash, she had jotted down a few lines from "You and Me" in a notebook. When she found her notes again, after Brian's death, she freaked out for a second. "It was like Brian had written the words; like he was speaking to me."

Realizing what her notes were, she went online and read the full lyrics: "Oh, and when the kids are old enough/We're gonna teach them to fly."

"When I hear this song," she said, "all I hear is Brian."

In that moment, I started crying. It hit me that we were all in this together. Brian was coming through in signs for all of us.

He was my husband and my partner, but he was not mine. It was a privilege to share time and space with him, as it is a privilege to share this time and space with my children—who aren't my possessions either!

I hadn't wanted freedom to come knocking the way it had; but it did. Brian never was mine, so I could let him go for whatever was next for him. He was free, and I was too. To move on to whatever was next for me, I had to fully surrender and let go.

In tragedy, there is a certain bind and a certain freedom, a liminality. Nothing is certain, in life or in death, but I believe that we all come from the source and return to it: love, salt, water, air, mineral, spirit, blood, fire, ash, and dust. We continue on, infinitely metamorphosing, floating through waves, flames, and clouds of one another. We belong nowhere, to no one, and everywhere to everyone at the same time.

Tahlequah is part of the officially endangered Southern Resident J Pod orcas, which live in the Salish Sea, between the United States and Canada. A memorial service was held in Seattle for Tahlequah's baby and there it was noted: *First we mourn, and then we take action.*

✳

Moving is an opportunity to shed what no longer serves us. In sorting through Brian's things, I triaged. I kept a few of his cozy sweatshirts and T-shirts, the ones I'd slept in every night for six months while cocooning. Mel still wears Brian's flannel shirt. Brooke wears his Harvard and MIT sweatshirts. Max wears his Canada sweatshirt and will one day literally step into his shoes—I saved him a fancy pair. Some of Brian's suits, I gave to his father, who wears the same size. The Walmart pants with the elastic waistband—those I gave to charity.

For the final walk-through of our California home, I sent the kids to the neighbors. The sun had set. The movers had picked up every last box, and every last dust mote had been vacuumed. The walls were bare. Our family photos would follow us east from the West Coast. A few would remain present and displayed in our lives forever, but others would be stored, maybe never to be unpacked.

Standing on the terrace, I looked out on Huntington Harbor. Brian and I had met near water, at Martha's Vineyard, and we had played and lived near water ever since. I inhaled deeply, turned, stepped inside, and pulled the sliding glass door shut behind me.

I walked through the kitchen, the dining room, the living room, the common areas where we had all gathered for three years—greeting, eating, talking, playing, doing homework, and grabbing snacks before heading out the door for school, work, dance class, or soccer practice.

Upstairs, where our bedrooms were, we had read, snuggled, said goodnight, planned for the future, and dreamt. Darkness poured in now through the master bedroom windows, stripped of shades and curtains. Standing in the doorway, I could see no trace of the cocoon we had built for ourselves and found comfort in. I sobbed for the fact the four us would never share a home with Brian again—no new memories would be built within these or any walls.

We were leaving our cocoon for a nest. In all the traveling and moving I had done, Maryland had always remained home base. I was born and raised there. Melanie, Brooke, and Max had been born back east, too. We were healed enough, but we still needed closer proximity to the extra secure and loving environment my immediate family provided.

In June 2012, closing the front door of our home by the Pacific Ocean, my hand felt electrified and my body, zapped. Save for the first week without Brian, closing that door marked the end of the single worst day for me. But it marked a turning point, as well.

Chapter Fifteen

As ready as the kids and I were for our fresh start, the house in Maryland would be—in my mind—a temporary holding place. It wouldn't be temporary in the way our cocoon had been, but everything was still very much up in the air, and, despite moving back to where I had grown up, we continued to ride out waves of emotions and adapting.

I called my former real estate agent to help us find another house. She was wary about showing us a place that was owned by a widow, only three doors down from where Brian and I had lived years ago, but when she walked Mary Kay and me through the home, a bottle of Three Sisters wine was sitting unopened on the kitchen counter.

"Of course!" we said.

The dead, as usual, were guiding and supporting me, sending me signs to go for it.

Our new house was built for a traditional family. There were two closets in the master bedroom and two sinks in the master bathroom—thankfully, there were no *His* and *Hers* towels. Still, I immediately set out to make the place our home. For the past fourteen years, I had consulted with Brian over nearly everything. There was freedom, now, in not having to ask anyone for input, but there was also great loneliness.

I wanted our new space to be totally comfortable and worry-free, so I imbued it with calm. By design, the place was not vibrant or eclectic. The kids and I lived, more or less, in a cream-colored dream. When a local friend visited us for the first time, she said, "It must feel so good to be back home. You must feel stable."

"Yes," I said. "Yes and no."

We want to believe in "the fix." We so badly want to believe we can work through a series of delineated steps when it comes to grieving, to "gain closure," a concept I don't fully buy into. Though I knew better, because of my experience losing Tricia, there were moments I wanted to force progress. But, though there may be typical stages in the grieving process, it is always amorphous and messy. A huge part of me felt overjoyed at being back home near family, but I was nowhere near fully settled or healed. I was healed enough, stable enough. This is, in part, why I wanted a home that was monochrome. Just landing there in its newness was enough. Who I was—the "I am" portion of the puzzle—was simply going to have to remain up in the air for a while longer.

We were beginning to want a new life, which in itself was progress. But mixed in was guilt over moving forward, and more so over the possibility of being happy again. With its colorless walls, our Maryland home reflected the blank but hopeful slates the kids and I were. Within these walls we could bring fresh eyes to all the puzzle pieces, to see how they had changed shape. We were the puzzle pieces—bright, unique, and in need of figuring out where we fit. What was our new arrangement? Even if the full picture we would strive to pull together was unclear, we could now at least pick up the corner pieces, and then the edges, and by paying close attention and experimenting, we could lock together the pieces of the frame.

The only thing we really knew is that our unfinished puzzle would not include Brian in the vital way it once had. We each still had a relationship with him, but physically he would be out of this picture. We proceeded like toddlers, with some clumsiness and caution, but also with eagerness and the will to forge ahead, to touch and know the unknown.

✳

Monumental tragedies force you to question who you thought yourself to be. The former you is no longer real, and who you thought you were going to be ceases to be possible. Rebirth requires a loss of security, certainty, identity, energy, and innocence. Before testing out new versions of "I am," I reflected on who I had been.

As Mrs. Brian David Robertson, I had most of it figured out. I was Brian's partner, I was the mother to our three children, and I was a founding partner of Evolution Workforce, working as a business coach for nutrition, fitness, and wellness entrepreneurs and executives. I had been successful at shining a light on my clients' blind spots, helping them see another perspective, and thus enabling them to take new action. Helping people become who they most want to be—whether it was Brian, my kids, my family and friends, or my clients—brought out my best self. When I was in this flow, my capacity to be an asshole diminished!

The married, mothering, and coaching Eileen is of course not who I had always been. Before I met Brian, I had reinvented myself countless times, in part because that's what many of us do in youth, but also because I wasn't satisfied with merely learning for learning's sake or landing a great job and calling it a day. My path had always been a multi-dimensional one and a huge experiment in "Who am I? Why am I here? What am I meant to do?" My journey has consisted of innumerable starts, attempts, trials, successes, failures, and test runs. None of it has been wasted; all of it has been transformative.

Since my early twenties, around the time I climbed Camelback Mountain in Phoenix and Tricia died, I have been on a journey—one that has entailed saying yes to many open doors and opportunities. Fresh out of college with a degree in management science, I said yes to a job in a cubicle documenting code that someone else had written. It was not my passion. I became restless.

In my mid-twenties, I toyed with the idea of becoming a hairstylist or a teacher. I'd dreamed of cutting hair and making people feel gorgeous since I was a little girl, and I wanted to inspire others, as teachers do. But the reality of having to support myself put those dreams on hold, and instead I pursued an MBA and got hired by Intel and then Amazon. I loved these demanding years, but I was so high-energy that the office space began to feel confining. Done with the traditional 9-to-always-later-than-5 gig and still trying to figure out what my life's purpose was, I worked on narrowing down and naming what I most liked doing. Some of this was simply a process of elimination, a "yes or no" level of decision-making.

I had always been an athlete who thrived on direct connection with others, so I studied and got certified to become a personal trainer. Before I got my first client, I injured my back and couldn't work out the way a trainer would need to work out. By this time, I was married to Brian, and I thought, "We're comfortable, so I might as well give my childhood dream a shot!" I enrolled in cosmetology school, graduated, and looked into buying a salon.

During my search for the right location to set up shop, 9/11 hit. Brian and I left for Mexico for a spell, and, while there, he got accepted to business school. It was clear we would be too unsettled for me to invest in a salon and become a brick-and-mortar business owner, so, back in the States starting that next summer, Brian began his studies and I tutored English, taught computer classes at Harvard, fitted wigs for cancer patients at the Dana-Farber Cancer Institute, and got pregnant with Melanie.

As soon as Mel was born, at the end of Brian's first year of business school, I went all in on motherhood. At the end of his second year, Brian took a job in Maryland and Mel helped us welcome her little sister, Brooke, into the world. I loved motherhood; I studied the shit out of it and imagined all the things our children would see and do. But motherhood for me was also a practice in not ruining them or killing myself in frustration.

After Max was born, I reinvented myself again. Wanting something simple because I had three little kids at home, I renewed my certification as a fitness trainer and began teaching boot camps in our neighborhood. I then studied and added a nutrition and coaching certification to my toolbox. In 2011, I was poised to take my work to the next level, combining my business knowledge with my love of guiding others toward their healthiest, most productive selves. And then my world imploded.

What follows the words "I am" changes. We marry, we transform; we give birth, we transform; we study whatever and create whatever, we transform. The list goes on infinitely, as does our potential. Transformation is sparked in the space between "yes" and "no." Sometimes it occurs swiftly, and sometimes it occurs over the course of many years through much practice. Transformation is sometimes sparked because of unfinished business. At times we seek it, at other times it comes for us. The very specific and painful opportunity to transform through Brian's death jolted me into becoming much more cognizant of and careful about the words I place after *I am*.

The concept of "I am" itself changed when Brian died. This time, my "I am," Eileen's "I am," was very much linked to the lives of three very young others. I became more aware than ever of *we* and its attendant *we are*.

I thought about how jigsaw puzzles are made. A puzzle factory prints a large image—whole—on its cardboard backing. The cutting machine cuts 300, 500, 1,000, or 3,000 pieces. The edges of these pieces are smoothed, and then the pieces are scrambled and boxed. We open the box and attempt to put together what already was. We reconstruct the preordained. A part of us is never 100 percent a blank slate.

Everything I had experienced up to the point of Brian's death had prepared me, in a way, for the aftermath of it. I knew how to reinvent myself, and, although nothing compared to the work I would have to do in that regard after he died, the truth is that I felt equipped enough to sit with the pain and work through it. People told me, "Of all the women this could happen to, we know you can handle this. We've seen you make the best of situations in the past, and we know you'll be okay."

Why didn't the worst of the bad days destroy me? Before Brian, I had made my own way, been self-sufficient. With him, I found an equal, a balance, a counterpart. After he died, I felt unbalanced, but I put my faith in the bigger picture. The kids and I were still here. We were meant to still be here, or we would have been on that plane with him.

CHAPTER SIXTEEN

As I explored who I might become, I often felt stuck and impatient. At a weeklong workshop on Whidbey Island in majestic Puget Sound—where Tahlequah and her orca pod continue to fight for survival—I met a woman who liked to work with metaphors. For obvious reasons, we hit it off.

I expressed to her my inclination to feel and act like a caged animal whenever I feel stuck. When the decisions I have to make overwhelm me—when I'm consumed with my purpose in life—I pace and growl in my cage, which is custom-built for me, in that I can stand in it and walk around. I can see through the bars of it but fear I might never get out.

Where is the key? What is it? I need to be the one holding it, damn it!

My metaphor-inclined teacher looked at me. She nodded. She asked, "Have you ever thought of lying down and resting in this cage in these moments you feel trapped? Have you ever thought of making yourself small, so you can escape it? Do you ask for help?"

What? No.

In caged animal mode, it never crossed my mind to chill. The animal in my cage screams, *I won't get what I want! I'll have to do things I don't want to do. I won't be in control. I won't get to play. What if I make the wrong choice? What if I fail? I don't want to be dominated by what I'm supposed to do. I am locked in!*

To call a locksmith—to think reasonably in the most desperate, uncomfortable, or inane situations—doesn't cross my mind. But in reflecting on what this woman said, I realized that, when pushed to the absolute extreme in the past, I did make myself small. I chilled out and surrendered instinctively, protecting and empowering myself and the kids in the process.

At a time when I believed I'd lost everything, including my freedom, Al Khuner showed up—the key, an angel. Family, friends, colleagues, and strangers helped. So what if chilling out, surrendering, and pulling in support might lead us all closer to our purpose?

Yoga teacher training had led me to where I needed to be. Asking questions—such a simple notion—helped immensely and empowered me to help others. Listening to my sister was also a key. Listening to my kids was a key. Slowing everything down—key! In the ongoing dismantling of who I was, a few locks had to be loosened more gingerly than I was used to. If I wriggled any key too hard in frustration, it would break.

My metaphor friend crossed my path during my ongoing struggle to figure out what I am here for, and she reminded me that releasing too intense a focus is yet another key—maybe *the* key—to figuring out next steps in regard to where we fit in this universe and what we are being called to do. All keys lock and unlock. They can cage us, and they can offer us freedom.

On my yoga mat, I know how to create an intention. I practice healing, gaining strength, and losing judgment. None are easy tasks. Finding the answer isn't easy, either, because, honestly, there is always more than one answer. There is always an alternate perspective, another story. I still am not entirely comfortable knowing there is bound to be more discomfort and more doubt no matter what choices I make, but I am working to welcome that discomfort and give it space.

When my head starts spinning, I attempt to slow down. I sit on a yoga mat and move through sun salutation or rest in child's pose. I get outside and walk. I breathe into compassion and work to forgive myself for not being able to recognize how attached I was to Brian until he was gone. I thought I knew all about being in the flow and letting things go, but until the cage dropped down around me, the knowing wasn't real. It was a practice, not an experience. The merger of practice and experience is what transformed me and what helps me find perspective again and again when I'm driving myself, or my family, crazy.

For decades, I was over-actively seeking *the one thing* I could be the expert on. In reality, life is not only about mastery, it is about practicing and continually learning. My role is to support the visionaries, the entrepreneurs, and the experts—who are also continually asking questions about passion and purpose in order to gain knowledge, to grow. I know through lived experience that, unless we radically accept the fact that there are some things we cannot control or change, without surrender and nonattachment, we cannot create anything new. If we are racing through our days, or our pain, we'll miss the signs the universe is sending us. Had I not slowed down and trusted that I was not alone, I wouldn't have been able to let in my next story. There would have been no space for Mike, nowhere for him to fit.

I know how puzzles work, and I want to help the families of geeks, inventors, pranksters, and genius creators stay fit together mentally, physically, and emotionally. I want families to fit together, through demands, challenges, disasters, and triumphs. When people tell me I am brave—when I actually believed in love again, for example—I said, "Thank you, but not really. Because what's the alternative?" My resiliency may have shown through after Brian died because I was born with it—we are all born with the potential to be resilient—but I have also had to practice rising from some low, dark, and painful places.

✳

The first summer without Brian, the kids and I flew from Maryland to Canada to visit his parents and to attend the third and final memorial service. It was held on his family's lake property, and it was beautiful, but to say that there wasn't a part of me that felt uncomfortable at not having been asked to provide any input would be a fib. The logical side of me understood that I was not part of Brian's original nuclear family and that everyone needed to celebrate his life and mark his passing in a way that healed *them*. Dave, Donna, and Julie were honoring *their* Brian. I really did not fit into this equation, and though my ego wanted to rear its bratty little head, I faced what my feelings of being an outsider meant.

Am I an out-law now, as opposed to an in-law? Will Brian's family still welcome me? Was their love for me bound entirely to their love for Brian? These questions were unfounded, but trauma and tragedy stir up fear and insecurity. We all were still raw that first summer, and I had to work hard to turn around my feelings of discomfort. The Robertsons had graciously been there and done so much for the kids and me over the years—starting with bringing Brian into this world and forming him. My "I am" wanted to kick its way back to "normalcy." And then I remembered, thank God, that this wasn't about me: this memorial was about Brian and his Canadian family.

Wow, I thought, finally. You can relax, Eileen. You aren't solely responsible for holding it all together and carrying forth Brian's memory.

At Brian's memorial in Canada, I was able to relax and listen to all the ways he was loved. I was reminded that we all suffer differently, and the kids and I were lucky to learn who Brian was as a son, a brother, a cousin, and a barefoot waterskiing buddy.

✳

It had taken me half a year to accept his ashes—they were foreign to me. They were scary. I asked my father to pick them up from the funeral home because I couldn't do it. He delivered them to

Brian's parents, and they took them to Canada. Dave and Donna were going to give me half that summer to take home to the States. I had decided that even if I did not want those ashes, the kids might. I wanted some for each of them.

Shopping for urns one night online, I imagined Brian laughing. For the most part, the urns were tacky. Some were monument sized—capacity: ten generations. Others looked like salt-and-pepper shakers. Grimly, I wondered if in the history of humankind someone had accidentally sprinkled ashes on their French fries.

Looking at the bag of ashes I was surprised. They kind of look like the ashes you find in a fireplace or after a beach bonfire. They looked like sand and dirt, earthly. They reminded me of what had struck me so purely the day I had stood beside Brian's casket: that we are spiritual beings temporarily inhabiting this plane. We are energy, and then dust. I thought I found a piece of Brian's Blackberry in his ashes. We are poetry and hi-technology.

I found a peaceful usefulness in Brian's ashes. Spreading them, we would remember him, and then we would literally let go. Ashes, memorial bricks, gravestones, and benches help keep palpable modern-day memories alive—keep those we lose alive in spirit. Julie spread some of Brian's ashes in the lake, while waterskiing. His MIT buddies would take their share on a hike up to Angel's Landing, in Utah, five years after his death.

Funny, but I never bought an urn. The bulk of my share of Brian's ashes remains in a box in my closet, next to a box of other memorabilia. Each of the kids has a small vial of ashes in their room.

✳

When Al, my funeral home angel, brought me to Brian's casket and asked me if I wanted his wedding ring, I did, of course, say yes. I instinctively put it on my finger. Brian's ring, the symbol of our marriage that he had worn for eleven years, was now secured on my finger by my engagement and wedding rings.

Our relationship as an earthly husband and wife was over, but I was not about to let go of our partnership and our promises to each other. We had kids to raise, for God's sake, and many other goals to accomplish together for this world. The three rings on my hand served as a visual and tactile reminder that, although I had no clue as to what our new relationship would look like, it was not over. Early on, I couldn't imagine ever wanting to take them off. I couldn't imagine ever introducing myself as anybody but Mrs. Eileen Robertson, Brian's wife.

But with time and the growing reality of the fact we were no longer an earthly husband and wife, I did stop referring to myself as Brian's wife and began to refer to myself as his widow. Eventually, looking down at our rings no longer provided the comfort they once had. Instead, they became a reminder of what was no longer possible. Still, I could not imagine taking them off. How would I do it? When would I do it? What would I do with them? They were beautiful rings.

New Year's Eve 2012 would mark—roughly—the one-year anniversary of Brian's death. It would mark what would have been our twelfth wedding anniversary. I decided this was when I would take the rings off, but as the date approached, I still wasn't comfortable and still didn't know what I would do with them. Maybe I could find a jeweler to melt the metal in them all together and make a new ring. I didn't know, so I did not let them go.

That Christmas and New Year's, a bunch of us gathered in Mexico. We built a bonfire. The rings around my finger, symbolizing no beginning and no end, caught its light.

I had brought a portion of Brian's ashes to our beach home, to share with our friends. They tossed some into the fire and later we took some on a hike to release at the top of our favorite mountain. Everything was about Brian that night—the flames, the warmth, the good group of people, and the laughter. The first time he and I had ever stepped foot on the property, he had stripped down to his underwear and jumped into the waves. The day after our big bonfire, Melanie and I went kayaking and saw sea lions playing in the waves. We tossed some of Brian's ashes into the Sea of Cortez, which Jacques Cousteau once referred to as "the world's aquarium."

After the kids and I returned home, I was sharing with a friend my struggle over taking the rings off.

"Eileen," she said, "have you ever thought of making a past, present, future ring? You could use your diamond as the center and put two stones on either side. One side would represent your past, and the other side your future. You can wear it on your right hand and never have to take it off."

It was the perfect plan. I could keep our three original wedding rings for Melanie, Brooke, and Max.

I went to a trusted jeweler and asked him to reset my diamond in a new setting, with December birthstones on either side. Brian and I got married in December and he died in December. Having this ring custom-made felt right. I asked that it be ready for Valentine's Day. I wanted to make the transition then.

On February 14, I removed Brian's wedding band, my wedding band, and my engagement ring.

Chapter Seventeen

In late February, I was at a girlfriend's house when my support coach called. Bob Mueller had been Brian's executive coach, and after the plane crash he had generously offered to take me on, pro bono. Bob had mentioned early in our call that he had some people he wanted me to meet—Jane in D.C., Mike in Chicago, so-and-so, and so-and-so. I made a note to call Jane and thought if I'm ever in Chicago, I'll ask Bob for more information on Mike. I had no plans involving Chicago in the near future.

At the end of the conversation, I told Bob I had taken my rings off, and said, "I'm starting to think about the possibility of meeting someone."

"Oh! That's why I think you should meet Mike."

Wait—what? What was his name? I wrote it down and after Bob and I hung up, my girlfriend and I Googled Mike. "He's hot!" we said in unison.

Almost every widow or widower I know admits to feeling guilty, to some degree and for one reason or another, when beginning to move forward or find romantic joy again. Even though our supporters have told us all along that our departed loved ones would want us to be happy, and even when we know that to be the case, guilt is sneaky. I felt guilty the first millisecond it struck me that loving again was possible; I felt confused—as in, good and bad, hopeful and sad, eager and hesitant—those first moments I allowed myself to linger in the possibility that there was another amazing man out there for me and the kids.

But I know a lot about love, and I believe in its abundance, its eternal capacity, and its ability to be found in the darkest places.

Conjure up one of your ex-loves—a wonderful ex. When you were in the process of ending things, it might have seemed there was nothing positive about that particular shared journey or its final destination, but with hindsight you know there is an oldie but goodie who really taught you something about the nature of love. Prior to meeting Brian, I'd been in a long-term relationship with a guy named Chris. Ours was a strong and empowering relationship, and when it ended, for a while I experienced what felt like a gaping hole in my spirit. That shit hurt. Breaking up is hard. But Chris came to Brian's celebration of life in California, and, when I saw him, the knowledge that I could love again pierced my heart, a shocking bolt of lightning. Proof was right there, in the form of this man I once loved dearly and parted ways with.

Barely a week had passed since we'd lost Brian, but death doesn't stop truth.

Of course, I would not and could not give that split-second notion of one day loving another man much thought at that time. All I could do was hug Chris, thank him for coming, and thank him for having let me go—an act that essentially made it possible for me to find and build a life with Brian. Chris was nothing but gentle, authentic, and generous in his condolences. We each carried memories of our shared time, and its impact, and so we carried part of each other—just as I would continue forth in my relationship with Brian. And, once I did meet another man, this man would understand what I meant when I told him, "Hey, I've still got a partner. I hope you're okay with that."

Wait, what was I thinking? Was it possible that there was any man out there as incredible as Brian? Someone who could love me the way he did—even when Scary Mommy and Hard-headed, Demanding, Selfish Wife surfaced? Would he understand it if he heard me say, "Go fix your own damn eggs, Melanie"?

Michael, the shaman in California, had said I would meet some preordained soul, and as time marched forward more people would cross my path and tell me to remain open, to be ready to receive. My story was not finished yet, as Eileen, as wife, or as mother. My story was always mine for the making.

But guilt—embarrassment—here it is: If and when I did find another amazing love and new daddy, and if and when we somehow merged our lives—I would cease to be a member of a very special club. Not many widows or widowers might want to admit this, but being cared for—cooked for, checked in on, and handled with care— feels good. Being the recipient of empathy feels really good. I'm not wishing widowhood or tragedy on anyone; I'm hoping it is obvious there are other ways to draw the concern or support we need without undergoing trauma. But the truth is, the kids and I had been so loved and helped throughout our grieving journey that, although we did not enjoy being part of "Club Bereavement," we had grown used to it. We had learned its language and customs. It had helped us gain new understanding and skills.

I felt terrible for thinking that, once I started dating again, once the world saw me taking a risk and kissing someone who was not Brian—then what?

Then.

What?

The dead are not the only ones who must face the unknown.

＊

I would meet Mike, in the flesh, in May 2013. Bob Mueller had been itching to set the gears of our connection in motion since early February, but other than the day of that initial phone call, when my friend and I had Googled Mike and had agreed he was attractive, I hadn't put much stock into anything panning out between us. For all of 2012, my sister Mary Kay had been my steady Friday night date, but, with my encouragement, she had gone off to teach in the Middle East. Now, though weekends could still be hard, I didn't think I was really looking for anyone to fill her Friday night shoes. The kids were engaged in school, dance, and soccer. My *I AM* explorations and exploits were a top priority. My attendance at a transformational course that would be held once a month over the next five months— that Mike, coincidentally, would also be attending that summer— was for me about further defining and following my life purpose.

Moving into the second year without Brian, I still sometimes wondered why I was still alive.

What work, what service, was I meant to be doing?

I went to the three-day transformational development conference as I always did—with no expectations, only an open mind.

And then . . .

Mike and I greeted each other and sat down together.

"Could this be him—the One? The one the shaman spoke of?" I thought. I was instantly buzzing like a middle-school girl.

"Am I nuts?" I also thought. "I could be wrong."

At that point, seventeen months after Brian died, I was okay with being nuts and wrong. First, because Mike was not available. Second, because I knew better than to be sure or right about anything. Third, another man—weird!

However, the mutual attraction on that first meeting was undeniable. We spent time together during the weekend participating in workshops and enjoying conversation over meals. When the weekend was over, the words I spoke when I said goodbye surprised me as much as they surprised him.

"If you become available and are interested in dating me," I said, "give me a call."

Who the hell was I?!

✳

That spring, Brooke had begun to deal with her grief more intensely, and though she insisted on getting through it on her own, I continued to assure her I was strong enough to handle her sadness as well as my own, Mel's, and Max's. Now in third grade, my middle child was stubborn and strong. To this day, when our entire household is taken out by the flu, it's Brooke who steps up and cleans up everyone's mess—despite being as sick as the rest of us.

Brooke regularly sought out the school counselor, and found a helpful spirit in her teacher, Mrs. O'Malley, a widow who had daughters and was remarried. Mrs. O'Malley and I had a heart-to-heart conversation on a field trip—to the Baltimore Museum of Industry.

Brooke hadn't made the connection when she brought home the field trip permission slip for me to sign, but I wrote to the school saying I wanted to join her on that trip. A few weeks went by. I had never been contacted, and I forgot I had signed on. When Brooke said one morning, "We're going on our field trip today," I asked, "Where?"

I don't know how I'd let it slip my mind. I sent Brooke out the door and called the school to tell them I would meet the kids there. When I pulled into the parking lot, "Someone Like You" came on the car radio.

I hung back from the chaperones and the leader of the pack, checking on Brooke from afar.

Mrs. O'Malley and I, the only two adults without a group of students to supervise, exchanged pleasantries. We followed the children around while the museum tour guide talked to them about the old oyster cannery and machine shops. In the Alonzo G. Decker Gallery under the airplane, we widows stood on the sidelines together.

"At some point," I said, "I'd love to talk to you about widowhood and your remarriage." I had just met Mike the weekend before, and had questions about widowhood and dating, but it didn't feel right to discuss the issue in Brian's memorial space.

"We can talk about it now," she said.

Um, okay then.

Mrs. O'Malley confirmed some of what I had already experienced. She drove home for me the idea that my kids were doing what many children in bereavement do—they were leaning on each other so that I could stay strong. There was one of me and three of them. The role reversal I'd experienced that first night with Mel, where she held my green Mala beads and assured me that we were all going to be okay, was a healthy phenomenon that might occur again.

"Your kids hide their true feelings from you because they fear losing you. When a new person comes and they know you're safe, they'll act out. The girls, especially, are likely to lose their marbles when you find someone new. You shouldn't wait as long as I did to let this new person in. You are young, beautiful, and you deserve to be happy. Your kids need and want a father more than they will let you know."

Tears came to my eyes. It felt like Brian was speaking directly through this woman. Who is to say why Mrs. O'Malley went on? The pep talk might have been as healing for her as it was comforting to me. Or maybe she was channeling Brian.

Mrs. O'Malley was an angel. She let me cry and sniffle, then went to Brooke's table and brought her over to me. I hugged my daughter and thanked Mrs. O'Malley before I said goodbye.

My brother and his wife had dedicated a brick in Brian's name to the museum. "Brooke," I said. "Do you want to find the brick Uncle Jimmy and Aunt Gina bought for us with Daddy's name on it?"

"Yes."

There are hundreds of commemorative bricks outside the museum, so we asked a museum employee to help us with our search.

"When did he die?"

December 22 was the date on Brian's death certificate.

"That's my birthday," the museum staffer said.

Of course it was.

We found Brian's brick next to the Esskay Meat Company brick. How fitting. I laughed. Brian had dressed up as a hot dog the Halloween before he died.

＊

A couple of weeks after my conversation with Mrs. O'Malley, I was holding an end-of-season soccer party for the kids and their teammates. The phone rang, but, as hostess with the mostest, I couldn't pick up. It was Mike.

When I called him back he told me he had broken up with the woman he'd been dating, and was available. I was excited. But what he said next shocked me. He'd had a dream: "We were at your place in Mexico with all of Brian's pals. Brian took me aside and said, 'I want you to take care of my girls and Max. But remember, I'm Max's hero. He idolizes me.'"

Holy crap! I could hardly believe what I was hearing, mainly because I'd had a similar vivid dream two nights before. In the dream, I had seen Brian and said, "I miss you so much."

"You don't ever have to miss me," he said. "I'm always with you."

I asked him what he thought about Mike.

"He used to be a jerk," he said. "But he's a good guy and you should go for it. And always remember I've got your back."

How had Mike dreamt about Brian too? Why? And how had he known it was him?

"Do you even know what he looks like?" I asked.

"Yes," Mike said. "I know what he looks like."

He had Googled him.

Mike was ready. I was ready. We made a plan, and then we made more.

Those who have been widowed or divorced know how weird these markers of "progress" feel—the first date, the first kiss. The returning rush of middle-schoolgirl energy and anticipation is freaky and a bit scary, but it's also fun. I hadn't been on a date with someone new since the summer of 1998. I hadn't kissed another soul since kissing Brian goodbye at the John Wayne Airport.

I reminded myself that Mike was a great guy, that Bob vouched for that, and, through that dream of mine, Brian did, too. And though I had just met him, I could also see it.

From June to August 2013, Mike and I were a couple in a bubble. We would meet in San Francisco with our transformational workshop cohort, then go out to dinner, just the two of us. We walked the hills of the city, getting to know each other. We held hands. I flew to Chicago and stayed at his place. We visited the Bean and walked the river. Those first few months, he witnessed no Eileen driving the kids to dance and soccer, no Eileen hanging out with other moms and dads. Over the course of the summer, Mike and I texted and talked on the phone like school kids—and then my kids started asking questions. As always, I was transparent with them. I told them there was this really nice, smart, fun guy, and that we were taking our time.

Later that summer, when I asked the kids if they minded my flying to Chicago to celebrate Mike's birthday, Max asked me not to go. I had recently returned from a workshop weekend out west, and he had missed me.

"Listen," Melanie said to Max. "If you want a new father, you have to let Mom go."

From the earliest days after Brian's death, Max, little boy that he was, had been gung-ho about my finding another daddy for him. He was on the lookout, scouting men in restaurants and parks, checking out tattooed men at the airport.

Before we moved from California to Maryland, the kids and I were eating at Panera, and I asked, "Can you imagine me ever getting married again and you having another daddy?" I knew what Max's reaction would be ("Yes, and he'll be awesome!"); but when the girls said, "Can we be in your wedding?" I started crying. That was the first time I had initiated an inquiry into my kids' need or desire for "another" father, and their unity and certainty astounded me.

While Mike and I were in the early stages of dating, before he met the kids, I asked them more than once, "Are you okay with this?" They were curious, and, except for Max, they were probably as nervous as I was.

The first time Mike flew in for a visit, Max came with me to the airport.

"We're going to pick up my new dad," he informed me.

"You don't know that," I said.

"Yes, I do. I'm sure."

I laughed, because clearly I had no control over this encounter. For all I knew, Mike would slide into the passenger seat, hear that he was "the new dad," and bolt up and out of the car right back through those revolving doors marked *Arrivals*.

I liked Mike and was having feelings he might miraculously be the real deal. Actually, I knew he was meant to be in our lives, but he wasn't as sure. He needed more time than I did to figure it out. *We live on borrowed time, dude. Trust me!* But I wasn't going to press it.

"What if you're wrong?" I asked Max.

"Well, I guess you'll keep looking and looking until you find one."

Chapter Eighteen

The weather in Maryland the day the kids met Mike was gorgeous. At the airport, as Max and I pulled up at Arrivals, I said, "There he is!" and simultaneously I thought, "What am I doing? Why am I at this airport right now? Is everybody ready for this?"

But I trusted my gut. There was nothing that couldn't be handled in conversation.

"Oh my God!" Max said. "He's so awesome. *He's so awesome!*"

I laughed. Mike slid into the passenger seat and the two gents introduced themselves.

"I knew you were going to be awesome," Max told Mike. "I can tell you're gonna be awesome!"

Everyone wanted to know who Mike was. My parents were waiting at home with the girls. When I arrived with Mike and Max, we all made some small talk, and then my parents left. Yup, no doubt about it: I was in charge of navigating the whole shebang. Was I going about this seemingly crucial first introduction the right way? Had I set it all up to make a lasting good impression? Was I in control of any of this?

Absolutely not. I had been checking in with the kids' minds and hearts for the past eighteen-plus months, but was everything going to hold? Or would it fall to pieces? Would anyone break down?

There we all were, mostly hopeful and excited, on that picture-perfect day. Mike went outside to fire up the barbecue. Another good man, good with fire.

From the kitchen window, like the June Cleaver I am not, I watched Mike throw a football with Max. When the girls beckoned to him from the trampoline, he hopped up and jumped around. Between washing the lettuce and chopping cilantro for guacamole, I reminded myself this was really happening. And, of course, Adele's "Someone Like You" came on the radio.

Yes, Brian was reminding me, *this is really happening. I've got your back.*

Everyone was well behaved that day. We talked easily, ate heartily, and played some more in the early autumn sunshine. But after Mike flew back to Chicago, the kids and I broke down in tears. What exactly was contained for each of us in those tears, I'm not sure I have the answer. I don't think we were crying because he left but because our house and yard had come so alive that we were reminded of what we had been missing.

Wow! It hit us: *That's what we want!*

What we wanted pummeled us.

Mike's first visit could not have gone any better, and, though the kids couldn't necessarily connect the dots and name it, I knew that, with his departure, they felt fear. I did, too. Our missing Brian came to the surface, became palpable in the light of this other man. The mere sound of a man's voice lifting into the trees, instructing little Max to go long for the ball; the weight of Mike's body—a body, nothing more, nothing less—bouncing my kids' smaller bodies up like Mexican jumping beans on the trampoline.

On visits to come, Max would accidentally call Mike "Dad" and then correct himself.

When Max caught us kissing once in the kitchen, he said, "I don't understand why you two don't get married."

Mike took most of it in stride. Understandably, friends of his were asking, "Three kids? Are you sure this is what you want?" Mike was a hot bachelor. He could take his time, have his pick, live in the perpetual fairy tale that "the perfect one" was out there, somewhere. And not that I ever considered myself chopped liver, but hey, I obviously came as a full-package deal. After Mike and I burst the Summer-of-Just-the-Two-of-Us bubble, time together meant time with the kids, driving them to various play dates, going out for pizza with them on Friday nights, and taking them to gymnastic and wrestling meets.

For Max, every visit seemed like an opportunity for Mike to pop the big question. Not that he harangued him about becoming his daddy and my husband, but the kid was looking out for us. At Costco one day, when I was off in the produce section and he had Mike alone in electronics, he asked him, "Why don't you marry my mom?"

Calm, cool, collected, and practical, Mike said, "I don't have a ring."

"Rings are over there," Max said.

Costco clearly caters to the modern romantic. Short of pricing them, my son had our diamond needs all figured out.

*

As for Melanie, after Mike came along she figured I was strong enough for her to lash out at again. Before Brian's death, we'd had our mother-daughter moments, mainly because she is so much like me. When she falls for something—bass guitar, skateboarding, rock climbing—her passion knows no bounds. Mel has to feel compelled or inspired to do what is asked of her, or she won't do it. She has never been inspired to clean up after herself. I get her. We bickered.

But after Brian died, especially when we were cocooning those first six months in California, arguments subsided among all of us. Mel stopped testing and prodding me. The girls were gentler with each other and with Max. Nobody had the energy to do battle. Death puts things in perspective—who on earth is going to pick a fight over whose turn it is to sit in the front seat this time?

Mrs. O'Malley had reassured me that the kids taking care of each other to some degree was normal and healthy. She forewarned me that the girls especially, because of their ages, might implode when a new man entered the scene. A teacher, a widow—she'd been right. The kids wanted a new father, they struggled with owning and accepting this desire, and they would attempt to push love away almost as soon as it came knocking.

Much of the pushing away was fear-based, but what can we do other than try to talk it through and let it ride its course? Melanie, Brooke, Max, and I all feared loving someone again as much as we loved Brian. If anything happened—no, no, no. None of us wanted to say it, but we all knew that anything could happen.

Mel lost her way and sank hard. The dark cloud of grief enveloped her with a great force that hadn't yet surfaced, though it was close to two years after she lost her father.

She went through a spell of trichotillomania, pulling out the hair on her head and eyebrows. This condition in pre-adolescence often overlaps with PTSD, anxiety, and depression. On her worst days, Mel would hide in her bedroom closet before school. On her best days, she would go through the motions. We put her on medication, which scared me because of what mixing meds had done to my sister Tricia. Did doctors and pharmacists pay more attention now? Had research, development, and communication on contraindications improved? I trusted Mel's doctor, but followed up with extensive Google research on everything she suggested and prescribed.

Mel and I went to therapy, together and apart. I needed guidance in helping her process her loss in the face of accepting what was looking to be a potentially huge gain for us as a family—Mike, the missing piece.

The kids and I had left our California cocoon; our work was done there. We were in Maryland to be closer to family and to start anew, but opening our arms to new love—to Mike—wasn't always barbecues, rainbows, and roses. Adding a new piece to our re-forming puzzle was exciting but discombobulating and stressful. Brooke only recently told me that she had been afraid to get her hopes up too high for Mike. Seeing the parents of several of her friends get divorced, she knew that the first "new person" at the door was often the rebound. My kids are wise beyond their ages.

How would Mike fit in, and for how long, young Brookie wondered.

For Mel, Mike becoming a regular and possibly permanent feature in our scene was a mixed bag. She was the eldest: she'd had more time with Brian than Brooke or Max. She sensed, as I had, and with as much confusion, that she would lose her status in that "special club" of fatherless children, the widow's kids. I don't recall her words exactly, but she spoke to the realization that, once we required less caretaking, we would become a regular family again. We would appear to be like everyone else.

For Max, at least then, Mike's inclusion was super simple. Mike was his new dad and we all needed to come around.

As for me, after Brian died, I would experience flashes of a strange remembering, as if everything that was happening was in fact preordained. The two of us had lived out our era, and Mike had lived single into his forties because he was meant to meet me. This is how it was meant to unfold for everyone. This is how I knew, through all the searing pain, that everything would be okay.

✳

Navigating three families—mine, Brian's, and Mike's—did not feel simple to me. Introducing Mike to the Robertson clan, especially, was bittersweet and awkward. Everyone had heard about him and knew the kids loved him. I loved him. Still, in the beginning, I felt extremely uncomfortable at times, worrying that seeing us happy with Mike would make others sad or possibly angry. Deep down, I knew the kids and I were loved by our families; I knew everyone wanted nothing but more love for us, but it wasn't always easy. The unspoken feeling sometimes seemed to be that this should not be happening. That Brian should be here.

Brian's parents, Dave and Donna, remained wholly generous as they went through their own pain and struggles. The first weekend they met Mike, I noticed they stayed down in the basement guest bedroom longer than usual before joining us, but who could blame them? This was the first Father's Day I was dating Mike, and they had come from Canada to visit. Throughout the day, watching the Orioles play the Blue Jays, or munching on snacks and catching their grandparents up on school events, the kids took turns sitting on Mike's lap. Was this too much, too "in your face"? I wondered.

I don't know what it was like for Dave and Donna that visit. I didn't ask, but I imagine that, since it was hard for me to watch, it must have been hard for them to experience. I also knew—they had said so more than once—that they wanted their grandchildren to be cared for and supported, and they could see we were in good hands.

Brian's family had always been incredible, and I loved him, in part, because of his roots and his people. After he died, I gave each member of his family even more credit—they were large-spirited and large-hearted.

✳

In the summer of 2013, Mike made the trek north to Canada with us—to Brian's family lake house, to their territory. Every year, the Robertsons hold a themed family regatta at their lake property, so Mike was going to meet everyone—Julie and her husband, Richard, their kids, cousins, distant cousins, aunts, uncles, and some of Brian's lifelong friends. As a water skier, Mike fit right in. He too had spent all of his summers at a lake. In so many ways, he took up right where Brian left off.

Not everyone saw it that way, I'm sure—and not everyone had to. What was interesting, instructive, and touching for me during our visit to the cottage that summer was the realization that I had been moving on with my life day by day, while simultaneously living each hour of each day with an awareness of Brian's absence—in a way others were not. I was not comparing anyone's grief or "progress moving forward" to mine, but it was clear that, as Brian's wife and partner of fourteen years, his sudden departure had been constantly before me—plain and simple. His place at the dinner table was empty.

People saw that I was happy now, which I knew they wanted, but I wondered if my being happy was too hard to witness. And because I am a work in progress, I was not entirely comfortable or sure what to do. Do I do *anything*?

My urge to fix things—to make everyone comfortable, to control and manage the unmanageable messy waves of sadness and longing—had to stop. I could not fix anything for anyone. The verb "to fix" means "to make something work better or to return something to its previously functioning state"; it also means "to set in place, to set in stone, to make permanent."

There is no permanence. There is no way to return a family who has lost one of their own to its previously functioning state. Our family unit was gone. I couldn't fix that. And yet here we were, clumsily trying to create a new one.

My yoga training helped me stay balanced and clear in Canada. People are going to do what they are going to do and feel what they are going to feel. Period. There are no rules in mourning and no time-lines for taking off a wedding ring, taking a chance on dating again after death or divorce, taking your life in a new, thrilling, scary, hold-on-to-your-horses-kids direction. I'd done so much work for myself and my kids. This newfound happiness and sense of wholeness is what Brian wanted for us. Look at his generosity, through his beautiful family, in sharing his beloved childhood vacation spot with this man, Mike.

The Robertson family regatta theme that year was Disney. I was one of those people who had never given Disney movies much thought—they were fairy tales, all with happy endings. But even Disney movies had their challenges, Disney characters their trials and traumas. Simba had the hard work of growing up after Mufasa died, Cinderella found selfhood in spite of her horrid stepfamily, and Nemo learned to keep on swimming in order to be found.

In 2014, the kids decided the four of us, plus Mike, would dress up as a family with superhuman powers. We were *The Incredibles*.

Who knew that pretending to be such a family—such a fairy tale—could come true? And who knew how much work it would be?

＊

In our clumsy first few steps of creating a new Robertson-Hamra clan, I think we sometimes felt we were pretending. Our fitting together seemed make-believe. Not fantasy fairy-tale make-believe, but the complicated, nerve-wracking, and awkward kind of believe-it-or-not situation of meeting your boyfriend's entire extended family for the first time while simultaneously managing three children's emotions and reactions to the big event.

There is probably a book on how to do this gracefully and well, but I didn't read it, and there we were, winging it.

In November 2014, Melanie, Brooke, Max, and I would meet the extended Hamra family in Springfield, Missouri—Mike's hometown, still home to the majority of his immediate family. I knew the potential merger with Mike would likely entail new family traditions and expectations. And, regardless of whether I liked unfamiliar customs or not, I knew there was pressure to conform to them for the sake of keeping peace.

We flew to Springfield the Wednesday night before Thanksgiving. Mike's parents greeted us graciously. Knowing that Mike's and my relationship was special but that we weren't engaged yet, Mike's dad, Sam, struggled to know how to refer to Mike with Melanie, Brooke, and Max. He ended up calling him Uncle Mike.

Making casual chit-chat, we discussed plans for the next day. We talked about what "our family" could bring to share, and then Sam mentioned that we should arrive by 2:00, so the professional photographer could take family pictures.

Photographs can be tricky territory. Immediately, I started to wonder what pictures the head of the family was talking about. Mike had made no mention of a professional photographer. Were the kids and I expected to sit for these pictures? I kept my questions to myself, but later asked Mike what was up with the short notice—the no notice at all? The kids and I hadn't brought any appropriate clothes, and, since it was now the evening of the day before Thanksgiving, I freaked out a little.

But of course, Walmart was open Thursday morning, and we went there.

I don't know how the kids felt, but I was nervous. I hadn't been nervous about meeting everyone, but what about this incredibly uncomfortable family photo situation?

Thursday, 2:00, at Chez Hamra, I noticed that *all* the pictures of their Thanksgivings and Christmases—through *all* the years— were displayed in huge formal frames across the living room walls.

If this relationship doesn't work out, and if we are supposed to sit for this photographer, I'm thinking: What will the Hamras eventually do with the Thanksgiving 2014 photographs? Photoshop them?

We laugh now, and nobody can see it in the photo, but I was sweating beneath that Walmart blouse.

We smiled and said cheese, though, and the family-building continued. When we sat down for dinner, it felt strangely like home. The food was familiar and delicious—Mike's mother had cooked a turkey, gravy, candied sweet potatoes, and a green bean casserole. There were at least eight different options for dessert. Beyond the food, the stories shared at the table were funny and relatable. Mike and I shared the same third-child spot in our sibling lineup, with the same brother-sister arrangement. The stories that Sam Junior, Karen, and Jackie told could have been the same stories that Jimmy, Mary Kay, and Tricia would have told. Mike's siblings had once stuffed him into a laundry basket and sent him flying down the steps. They tried embarrassing him by exaggerating digestive issues caused by eating too much cranberry sauce.

Melanie, Brooke, and Max got a kick out of exploring Mike's childhood bedroom, which was almost entirely intact from his childhood. A huge Curious George stuffed animal sat on a shelf. Melanie and Brooke were curious Georges about one particular photo they found on Mike's wall. Back in the good old days, Mike had been a strapping local catalog model. There he was, shirtless and surrounded by three cheerleaders, clearly striking a late-'80s, early-'90s pose. And wearing the hairstyle to match.

"Does my mom know about that picture?" the girls asked, not so subtly reminding him that they had my back.

The kids had fun playing with their instant "potential cousins," and although the Hamras were all incredibly lovable, there was still an inkling of a feeling among us—the Robertsons—that we weren't quite with "our" family. We couldn't instantly love these people, despite feeling we should be able to. Thanksgiving 2014 reminded us that cocreating relationships takes time, and successful mergers don't happen overnight. Over dinner and laughs, we felt warm, comfortable, and satisfied, and knew that, with patience, we could make it work if we wanted to.

❋

It's ironic that Mr. Incredible's struggle at the start of the original movie is to fit in and maintain his cover as a regular guy. Mike was an incredible, eligible bachelor: intelligent, fit, funny, kind, driven, successful, attractive, no kids, never married, and in his early forties—you get the picture. Me, I came as quite the package myself: single mother of three kids—all of us, in my mind, incredible, but admittedly we were still working through some pretty heavy stuff. Why would a guy like Mike choose to become husband to a minivan-driving mid-forties-something woman with scars from three C-sections and breasts that had nursed three babies? Why would he choose to become "Insta-Dad" to two tween girls and a rambunctious little boy?

I asked myself these questions, but I had not been the only one asking them, for sure.

In the initial stages of our relationship, some of Mike's friends and family were not huge fans of our dating. When they first got wind of the full story, they asked him, directly, "What are you trying to be? Their savior?" They said, "You have your pick of women who are young and have no children." They reminded him, "You have always wanted kids of your own. Do you think Eileen *really* wants another? She's too old to have another, for crying out loud!"

The voices from the outside were not always entirely different from the voices in Mike's head—I know this because I felt it, and because he told me. He asked himself if he was in love with me, or if he was a man on a rescue mission. He loved the kids, but that also implied or demanded that much more consideration, that much more of a commitment. I fully believed he was our perfect fit, and I could feel when his faith was being tested. Mike strayed in his mind often, and once, in fact, he did stray. He went on a date with a woman in the midst of our long-distance semi-complicated and scary early days. Loving me, Melanie, Brooke, and Max was a huge undertaking, and at times it was not comfortable. In the face of it all, one time, he sought escape.

Fortunately, Mr. Incredible's trip back to Bachelor Land was short and relatively inconsequential. Our guy saw it isn't any super-power that keeps the world spinning, it is family—and he had found his.

CHAPTER NINETEEN

"Wow. Holy crappo, they're getting married!"

Mike and I were wed in January 2016, in Chicago. It was cold, and I wore white.

In her "holy crappo" wedding speech, Melanie said, "I'm going to share with you something personal. I'm not a crier. I don't normally cry when I get sad. When I saw them walking down the aisle, I happy-cried. . . . I think it makes all of us happy to see them together."

The night before, at the rehearsal dinner, she said, "I could say a lot of things tonight, but tonight, this toast is about Mike. To Mike.

"When Mom first talked about starting to date, I wasn't interested. You kept calling and texting her, and I was like, 'Great, who is this guy?' I wanted to know you, because I was worried. You hear all those stories about awful stepfathers; you know what I'm talking about. And then I met you, and you were good, but I was still like *whatever*. I was not interested in having you be my dad.

"Over the past two years, you showed me you aren't like most adults—you really listen to me, you care about what I think, you care about what my sister and brother think. You care about us.

"I'm just so happy my mom found you and that you are going to be my new father figure. I know my dad would approve."

There was not a dry eye, at either event, after my older daughter spoke. I could not be prouder of my children.

At our wedding, so many of our guests spoke of the importance of family. Mike's father, who joked that he had been waiting a long time for his son to take the leap into marriage, talked about the great fortune it is to forge "one big family."

My sister Mary Kay said, "This is all about family. Acknowledging family—extraordinary families—however they're created. So, here's to the Fab Five!"

Brian's sister, Julie, stood up from the Robertson family table and thanked Mike directly, for making me, Melanie, Brooke, and Max so happy.

After toasts and dinner and cake were over, it was time to dance. Mike and I took the floor to "Lucky" by Jason Mraz and Colbie Caillat.

I am Irish, I am lucky, I am Eileen Robertson Hamra, and we had instructed the DJ to "put the needle on the record" before our first dance as a couple was finished so that the kids could join us for a first dance as an official family.

The five of us, happy and dressed fancily, followed Brooke's choreography to Rihanna's version of Calvin Harris's song "We Found Love." Guests were smiling so hard at this point, I am sure their faces hurt. And then, to everyone's added delight, we began dragging them out on the dance floor to party. Together, Mike, the kids, and I were the Fab Five, and we had a fairy-tale wedding. Today, against a whole lot of odds, we are *The Incredibles*—plus one.

✳

Back when we had first started dating, Mike asked if I was interested in having kids. I said no. "I already have three, and unfortunately a fourth isn't possible." After Max was born, I was so 100 percent entirely no-doubt-about-it dead-set *sure* I did not want ever to get pregnant again that I had my tubes tied—right there, after my third C-section.

I joked with Mike, telling him that if he wanted kids he could have mine because, "It turns out, they're in the market for a dad."

Saying no to having more children wasn't necessarily because I didn't *want* more kids, but because I was absolutely positive it was not possible. If I could wave a magic wand and, *poof,* a little Mike and Eileen could pop up, I would be all for it.

I know some women love being pregnant—they feel radiant, beautiful, and purposeful. Not me. Pregnancy hormones zap my energy and make me feel as if an alien has entered my body. When I'm pregnant, it is a very long nine months for me and everyone around me.

Even if I could get over hating being pregnant, I was sure having another baby might kill me. I was in my forties and had already had three C-sections. I didn't think my uterus and body could handle another baby. The first C-section was necessary because Melanie was breech. We tried turning her around, but as a foretelling of her strong-willed personality, she wanted to come into this world "her way." Finally, my obstetrician took charge.

With Brooke, I intended to take the natural route, but she was late. This concerned the doctors, so they scheduled a C-section. After my second surgery, any subsequent babies would also have to be delivered via C-section.

If my body could handle being pregnant again, tubal ligation did complicate matters. The doctor had said, "If you ever change your mind, you can always try IVF."

I'd said, "No way in hell will I ever do that!"

First of all, the third kid is a charm. Second, no more freaky hormonal surges for this gal, thanks. Last, I am not a medically oriented person. Doctors, needles, and prods to my body make me a little crazy. I have almost passed out at my yearly check-up.

I had Max at thirty-seven, which is considered a high-risk maternal age. In addition, I'd had two miscarriages between Brooke and Max, one of which was due to a chromosomal abnormality. I knew this because it was identified after I had a dilation and curettage.

Max was a blessing, and I was done. Brian and I had been blessed with three healthy children and our baby-making journey had reached its end. Mike might not have a biological child of his own yet, but he was proving to be a patient, warm, fully engaged father figure to Melanie, Brooke, and Max.

✳

Throughout our courtship, Mike stressed that having a child was important to him. I really didn't think I could. It was probably *the* question, *the* conversation, we had to get through if we were going to make *The Incredibles* a real-life fairy tale. And then I took a call from one of my favorite coaches, Debbie delaCuesta.

Debbie had been supportive of me through my entire journey—since I had first reached out to her with questions about raising the kids through grief and without Brian. On this call, she rocked my world when she said something to the effect of, "What if exploring having a baby is something you need for your relationship and your family? What if everything you are telling yourself about it not being possible is simply your assumption, and not the truth?"

"Holy shit, Debbie," I said. "Are you saying I should actually explore having another child?"

"I'm just saying—"

Okay, but what did she mean we might need another baby for our family?

Mike and I had a lot going on. We lived with one foot in the fairy tale and the other in mega-adjustment mode, trying to fit together our puzzle. To add another freaking piece was something I had to sit with. Impossibility . . . to improbability . . . to what? I would have to turn it all around. I would be turning it all around.

And so I let my mind and heart explore the reality of trying to get pregnant again, of having another baby.

There was some practical risk assessment to be done. For the sake of exploration, I set up a doctor appointment at a well-known

Maryland fertility clinic. Appointment after appointment, as test results came back, it seemed Debbie had been right, and what I had assumed had been wrong. It was not impossible for me to conceive and carry to term. Risky, yes, but my body and uterus were healthy. A slim chance, though. The probability of having a child with my own eggs was less than 2 percent, but it wasn't impossible. With donor eggs, specialists said, I could almost certainly get pregnant.

So what would a new baby mean to our family?

Maybe having a baby would help us to stop trying to figure out how to fix the unfixable and instead to create something new—a new family. Maybe this new baby, born against so many odds, would emerge with superpowers and be exactly what we all needed and wanted: the alchemist baby, filling in the cracks where our family had been broken—the baby as gold, the baby as glue. The *kintsugi* child.

Mike and I talked about the science and medicine of it all; we had many heart-centered conversations. I was willing to try to give Mike what he really wanted, but I knew what he wanted was not only for him, it was for us. The minute the kids and I landed in Chicago, I found an amazing doctor, Dr. Angeline Beltsos, to guide us through our fertility journey. Her positivity and optimism made it feel real, that with her guidance it would be possible to turn the impossibility of pregnancy toward and beyond the improbability of pregnancy. Under this woman's care, I could turn it all around.

At first, I wanted to get the show on the road and use donor eggs, because that was the "surest" and quickest route to pregnancy. But then I slowed down so that we could look at what we really wanted. Mike and I wanted a little Mike and Eileen, and so, even though succeeding at making our mini-us wasn't probable, it was not impossible. It was worth giving it a shot. And so, the yearlong IVF journey began.

From October 2015 through April 2016, we did three rounds of IVF with my own eggs and one mock round that involved more testing. Anyone who has been through IVF can tell you the process requires hundreds of shots, countless doctor appointments, sonograms, blood tests, and many hours filled with hope and disappointment. With each test and sonogram, you anticipate and hold faith that everything will come back with data—awesome, miraculous data—that will indicate that you are closer to reaching your goal of having a baby.

We got lucky. On the third round of IVF using my own eggs, we received the prized statement "You are pregnant!" only to find out a few days later that my hormone levels indicated the pregnancy would eventually fail. I wasn't surprised. I had been able to produce a lot of eggs for my age, but the quality of them was an issue. Becoming pregnant, finding the right mix for success, would be like finding a needle in a haystack.

After that pregnancy, I felt strangely accomplished. I had been pregnant with Mike's and my child, even if only for a little while. I was forty-five, and my body and ovaries had done their best, but now it felt right to move on to donor eggs. We wasted no time finding a donor and tried our first donor egg round in June 2016. Much to our surprise, that round failed. We quickly found another donor, but then decided we needed a short break from IVF. My body and our spirits needed to recover.

We took the month of July "off," and feeling fresh in August, I went to the baseline appointment for my next round of IVF using donor eggs. Without going into all the medical details, one thing the doctors tell you at this appointment is how many of your own eggs you have growing. On August 8, 2016, I had sixteen follicles—a record number for me! I thought to myself, *one of those eggs has got to be viable.*

After my appointment, at lunch with my new friend Nina, I could barely eat or pay attention to our conversation. I kept thinking, *maybe I should try one more time. Maybe.* Stabbing at my salad, I couldn't contain myself. "Listen, Nina, I know we don't know each other all that well, but I've been trying IVF for a year . . . and now I wonder what I should do . . . if I should try one more time. With my own eggs."

She looked at me and said, "Maybe I'm biased about the genetics, but I think you should give it one more go."

That was all I needed to hear. I picked up my phone and texted my doctor. She called back immediately, agreeing it was worth a shot. I left Nina that day and drove to the pharmacy to buy the required medications—you seriously need two grocery shopping bags for all of them—that would stimulate my ovaries one more time in hopes of having our "golden" baby.

A few days in, I began to doubt myself and to think that I had been a fool. I had acted impulsively: This giving it another try was a huge waste of time and money. But then again, we had started down the path and I might as well finish. No point in quitting now. Egg retrieval was set for August 24, on my forty-sixth birthday. The number of eggs we retrieved of the sixteen possible was eight, and only three had fertilized "normally." The numbers were not great and now I was certain we were wasting time. But—Happy Birthday to me, let's make a wish—I would go through this process to the very end.

On the fifth day, after you retrieve and fertilize the eggs, you are supposed to find out how many are "good enough" for genetic biopsy. The call came: two were still growing and not quite ready. If the process wasn't brutal enough on my body, it was tough on my psyche, too.

The next day, on Mike's birthday, we got the call that we had one egg that looked healthy enough to biopsy.

"Just do it!" we said, foolish or not.

Doctors sent the biopsy to the lab and then froze our one chance at a miracle.

We waited for the lab to do their thing.

The waiting during IVF is a special version of hell—talk about not knowing and wildly wanting to know. As much as I tried not to think about it, it was all I could think about. For two weeks, jacked up on hormones, I stayed as busy as possible but couldn't stop the IVF tsunami in my mind. Yoga didn't help. This was rollercoaster time.

Thankfully, though, time marched forward. I was walking in the door from running errands when Dr. Beltsos's name popped up on my caller ID. Most of the time, her nurses called me with results or follow-up questions. When I answered, Dr. Beltsos said, "Eileeeeeen . . ." Without her saying another word, I shouted, "No way!"

"Yes way, Eileen!" And we giggled with excitement.

I started happy-crying. I couldn't believe it, and neither could she: I was the oldest patient she had ever had with a healthy, viable embryo.

My excitement, joy, and amazement turned to sheer panic within a minute of receiving the news. The embryo—our embryo!—was still nothing more than a bunch of cells sitting in a freezer. It had to survive being defrosted, survive the transfer, and survive in me for months before it would really be our dream come true. The next few weeks of preparing for embryo transfer turned into an obsession about how to get this baby to "stick." My sister and I joked about chewing gum as a way to control the process. We chewed a lot of gum.

This baby had a chance, but whether everything would work out wasn't really up to us. I had learned this lesson already and was doing my very best to channel surrender. When the day came for the transfer, the nurse, with the paperwork of our grade 6AB embryo in her hands, said "Mike and Eileen, you found the needle in the haystack. And it's a boy."

The hundred-cell embryo became even more real. Mike and I watched the monitor, as the nurse transferred our baby boy from the petri dish to my womb, with every prayer sent out to any being who would listen.

CHAPTER TWENTY

After the transfer of our little guy—our miraculous clump of cells—I came home and didn't want to move for days. All I wanted was to make sure the little guy was burrowing into his home for the next nine months. One of the lovely things you get to do when going through IVF is to stick your butt with 2-inch-long needles full of progesterone, one of the key hormones needed to sustain a pregnancy. Five days after the transfer, you return to the doctors for bloodwork. At this time, it is usually too early to tell if you are pregnant, so they only test for progesterone.

Me being me, of course I decided to take a home pregnancy test that morning: negative. I was really bummed, but maybe it was too early. I went anyway to the doctor, got my blood test done, and then had coffee with Nina. While Nina and I were chatting about our future business plans and trying to keep my mind off being or not being pregnant, my phone rang. It was the nurse telling me that they had done a special high-tech pregnancy test. I guess they couldn't wait, either.

Positive!

I was pregnant with a miracle.

Mike and the kids were so excited. And then there was the nine months of dealing with me pregnant. I won't go into the excruciating details, but suffice to say, no one ever wants to see me pregnant again. If we could, we would all take a little amnesia pill to magically erase the havoc my hormones inflicted on the family. Thank God everyone forgives me!

Being pregnant at forty-six was not smooth sailing. Making sure that baby Hamra was hanging in there and growing required more tests than I like to remember. Zack has more pictures of himself in utero than Mike's dad, aka "Sam Camera," has ever taken.

Our baby was scheduled to be delivered on June 23, but at our doctor's appointment the Monday before, the ultrasound tech asked me if I had gestational diabetes.

"No," I said. "Why do you ask?"

"Your baby is measuring really big. Like over eleven pounds."

Ultrasounds are never 100 percent accurate, but if believing this baby was that big would mean getting him out of me sooner, I was game. The doctor came in and said, "I'm moving up your appointment from Friday to Wednesday. He's ready."

At 4:00 a.m. on Wednesday, June 21, summer solstice 2017, Mike called an Uber driver to take us to the hospital to have our baby boy. When we arrived at the hospital, Mike realized we had forgotten the cord blood kit at home. We would be saving and storing some of our baby's blood for any future need. The scheduled surgery was not for another two hours.

"Go back and get it," I told Mike. "I'll check in and wait for you."

I breathed in, I breathed out, until Mike returned.

"You are never going to believe what our Uber driver's name was," he said.

I waited for it. I had no doubt it was going to be good.

"Allah," Mike said.

Seriously, God had driven us to the hospital to have our baby on the summer solstice. The angels had our backs. Zack weighed in at eleven pounds, five ounces. The nurses had gasped. "Umm," one nurse said, "we have to get a conversion chart for this guy." Nobody had known what 5,000+ grams converted to in pounds.

Zack really was Incredible!

✳

The first time the kids got to visit Zack at the hospital, they did not want to leave when visiting hours were over. "Mom, I love him so much," Mel said. "I didn't know I would love him this much."

Brooke was a natural with her baby brother. Max had to sit—with an adult close by—to hold him. This baby was a giant when he lay across *my* chest, so adult supervision was necessary.

Zack is the glue; his super power is bonding us all together. This kid brings laughter to our house. He dances with Brooke; he climbs—like Melanie, with no concept of boundaries; and he worships his big brother. Zack could watch Max unload the dishwasher all day if we let him. It is obvious he is trying to grow up as quick as he can to keep up with his siblings. Our dog, Buddy, whom we rescued when we moved to Chicago, thinks Zack is his puppy, and sticks close to him.

There is a great risk in saying some of the things one might think when they have lived through experiences like this. Saying "Brian's death was a gift," can be easily misunderstood. But what we experienced after his passing was a gift. Zack would not have been possible without Brian dying. Everything did turn out better than okay. We are a lucky family.

Chapter Twenty-One

I have mentioned a scene that played out, just outside the Baltimore Museum of Industry, before Brian's first Celebration of Life. One of our previous nannies, Lindsay, found Brooke sitting alone in the lotus position atop a concrete block: her eyes were closed, her little back was straight as a ruler, and her hands were resting, palms up, on her knees in *shuni mudra* (which unites space and fire and helps provide emotional stability). The lotus flower is a Buddhist symbol of purity and faith.

Lindsay took a photo.

Science and spirituality show that practicing yoga and meditation changes the neural networks of our brains; stimulates glands, nerves, and organs; grounds and energizes us. As we practice, learn, and transform, whether we ever sit on a yoga mat or not, it is possible for all of us to become like the lotus flower, which, though rooted in mud, floats beautifully on the water's surface, opening to the sun.

In November 2018, I received an email from my father. He doesn't usually communicate via email, so I was curious. With some encouragement from me, he had been taking a gentle yin yoga class for a couple of years. One day after class, he decided to attend his first meditation session, where the teacher asked participants to sit in lotus position with palms facing skyward.

"The last time I saw this position," he wrote in the email, "was when Brookie was doing it in the parking lot before Brian's Celebration of Life in Baltimore. I was in tears during the whole session."

He attached to his email the photo Lindsay had snapped. I hadn't seen it in years.

My father's Knights of Columbus chapter supports a philanthropic foundation that builds schools, medical dispensaries, and wells for villagers in northern Tanzania. Thinking about their basic needs not being met, he ached, and he ended his email by asking if we might want to raise funds together as a family, to build a well in Tanzania to honor Tricia and Brian's memory.

After saying yes, I stared at Brooke in that photo and thought not so much about the day the picture was taken, but about how far all of us had come, how much we had learned together, as an ever-loving and ever-evolving family.

Don't misunderstand me. We aren't perfect in our quest to live with a keen awareness of the preciousness of time. We function on autopilot sometimes. We go through spells where we forget to be cognizant of, and grateful for, the lessons, the love, and the light we absorb and reflect. Like most people, we are not "professional" meditators or spiritual gurus and can't always be in the moment or be appreciative of *all the moments*.

When shit hits the fan, though, autopilot fails and the narrative ruptures. The simplest things—good butter on good bread, the comfort of a warm shower—may be all we need to come back to the present.

Eventually, without dwelling in the past and wishing things were *as they once were*, we can appreciate all the ways we've created and sustained a real "fairy-tale" life.

Last summer, the summer of 2018, Max's teachers nominated him to attend a summer leadership camp in Washington, D.C.—a fairly big deal. At first, he said he wanted to go but then changed his mind. He was begging me to let him skip it. I asked Mike what he thought and wondered what Brian would do. It seemed like the right thing for him to go. "If you give it a shot and really still hate it, I will come get you," I told Max.

He was only ten, and summer camp should not feel like torture.

Balancing somewhere between trying to reduce the pressure of following in Brian's genius-directed footsteps and telling our kids, "To whom a lot is given, a lot is expected," we hope our children comprehend their fortune in having the brains, the family, and the opportunities they've been given. We tell them on a regular basis that, if they pursue what they love to do, everything will work out; but we know—because my kids write and talk about these things still—that polarities exist. Brian was doing what he loved when he died. Their father was kicking ass, firing on all cylinders, showing up for those who mattered most, and still . . .

So, Max does go to leadership camp, and he calls me. He's not thrilled with it, but there is one kid there who, like him, respects boundaries and time. Max and this kid tell each other, "I don't want to talk. I want to read." They get each other. And then Max tells me this: "Mom," he says, "The best part of camp so far is the movie we watched: *Endurance*."

Pre-parenthood, Brian and I once visited the Antarctic. Prior to traveling, I read Irish-born explorer Ernest Shackleton's story, *Endurance*. As a parent, I always told the kids, "You have to read this book. We have to watch the movie." But you know how it goes— they had music, dance, and soccer practice. Still, the story kills (astounds?) me: How do you climb a mountain made of ice, survive even ten minutes in icy water, not freak out completely after floating through one dark night in that sea?

"These guys put nails on the bottoms of their shoes and made it," Max says. "The will to live can help you get through anything."

Isn't that the truth? Sometimes all you are left with is your will to live.

Grief is a long haul. Our family didn't drive nails into the bottoms of our shoes to survive it; we endured by holding each other as tight as puzzle pieces and promising each other in various spoken and unspoken ways that we would be okay.

✳

Brian hadn't intentionally set out to become a rock star in the solar industry: He initially turned toward the idea of installing solar panels at our place in Mexico for the same reason he wanted to become a pilot and fly his own planes—because of our home's remoteness. Brian learned solar science by applying it, and then it hit him: *With alternative energy we can help reverse some of the damage we've done to this planet—for our kids, for the future.*

He was a creative businessman, a caring scientist, and a down-to-earth spiritualist. Our whole family looks for ways to continue this energy and spirit in small and big ways. From 2012 to 2017, I was the chairman of a joint venture between the Brian D. Robertson Memorial Solar Schools Fund and the Solar Foundation. We designed a vision that would be worthy of Brian and called it "20/20 Vision of Solar in America." The aim of our collaboration was to facilitate the installation of 20,000 solar energy systems at K–12 schools throughout the United States by 2020. Okay, that was way more than we could realistically do, but we worked toward it, anyway, and made a difference doing it.

I needed to step down from leading this joint venture when Zack, the latest piece of our family's legacy, was due to arrive. There are times when you cannot do it all.

Our family has done smaller, more personal things in Brian's name too. This may sound insignificant—and unhealthy—but every August when we are all together in Canada, we order and devour boxes full of Dixie Lee Chicken to celebrate Brian's birthday. Brian loved that stuff, famous in Canada since 1964, and I'd played a joke on him once by replacing the thighs, legs, and breasts of his order with vegetables.

On Facebook, on the one-year anniversary of his death, I started a *What Would Brian Do?* thread.

Add salt.
Blow something up.
Channel Will Ferrell.
Dance with his daughters.

There is an element to legacy—or rather, to the "how to" of carrying it on—that can be confusing. Social media, as always, simplifies and complicates matters. But, just as there is no right way to grieve, there is no right way to carry on someone's legacy. There are no clear lines, no dates set in stone, no shoulds or musts. Do what feels right for you and your loved ones, and remember it is never too late.

Tricia's friends inducted her into the Water Polo Hall of Fame twenty-five years after she passed. Mike, Max, Zack, and my nephews were present at the ceremony. Tricia died way before the kids were born, but they now have a modern-day memory of her. They have a way of knowing someone so special to the family that they wouldn't have had otherwise.

After Tricia died, I watched my mom as she dealt with photos of her. How many photos do you keep up on the wall in that first year? Five years later? Twenty? Which photos remain visible, while so visibly fixed in time, and which do you relegate to a good old-fashioned photo album or a shoebox? A year after Mike and I were married and I was already pregnant with Zack, my mother still had Brian's and my wedding picture prominently displayed on the mantel—the spot for the most important photos. I doubt Mike ever noticed, but a few months ago I asked if we could at least add a picture of Mike and me. Of course, my mother said yes. She kept the picture of Brian and me up as her reminder of the love that brought three of her precious grandchildren into being.

There are no hard and fast rules concerning any of this "grief etiquette," beyond this: You do you.

Even the Queen of Letting Go, as I call Marie Kondo, instructs us in *Tidying Up* to wait to let go of sentimental items until after we've practiced asking ourselves loads of times, "Does it spark joy?" When deciding to hold on to something or to let it go, we practice first with things that hold less personal value, such as unworn skirts, unread books, or travel-size bottles of shampoo.

Sentimental items such as photographs and gifts, Kondo says, are the last items to approach. Guilt, it seems, takes up space in our homes.

"Keeping an item beyond the time it sparks joy for you," Kondo says, "will only diminish the care and appreciation you have for the other items in your life."

I believe in the infinitely expansive nature of giving and receiving love. Our souls, in their interconnectivity, have more room to grow than we know, but she's right. Our possessions can contain and emanate love for only so long. Items that meant so much to the giver and the receiver at one time were a gift at that specific time only. Letting go of a present a loved one gave me does not equate to tossing out the memories of joy associated with it.

Marie Kondo seems to think about space the way Brian thought about time—it is precious. Fill it thoughtfully and wisely to live your best life now.

Letting go is as much a part of legacy as deciding what to carry forward.

Chapter Twenty-Two

The true power in living a good life today and leaving an impactful legacy shines through in acts, not in things. The laughter my kids share with their cousins over a meal of greasy fried chicken in Canada is priceless. The ongoing work people are doing in renewable energy, cancer research, and fertility changes lives. When I found Brooke watching YouTube videos of Brian speaking at various conferences, she told me, "I was starting to forget his voice. I remember what he looked like, but I wanted to hear his voice and see him in action again."

Something remains after death, even if we aren't entirely sure what that something is or does. "We are continuous energy," American poet Mary Oliver told *On Being* host Krista Tippett in 2013, and this is why "we bury a dog in the garden with a rose bush on top of it."

For Oliver, "[The afterlife] is never nothing."

The quest for knowing God or explaining the mystic and wondrous, the attempt to find the words to describe one's spirituality, the unearthing of one's calling, Oliver also thought, is never-ending: "What you end up believing, even if it shifts, has an effect on the life you live, the life you choose to live, or the life you are trying to live."

I have always believed what Mary Oliver believed, and I didn't know it until after she died and I listened to her.

Long before Mary Kay and I went on our sisters' trip to Ireland to give Tricia her bench, I trusted in something larger than the sum of us. I believed in fairies and angels. Energy is shared; we are but little bundles of it, all mineral, water, and stardust. As strong, stoic, or independent as any of us are, we are never alone, because the laws of physics dictate we cannot be alone, we are not meant to be alone. We are all connected and simultaneously living and dying, cyclically discovering gaps in our experience and growing to fill them.

When you walk through the front doors of our home in Mexico, your feet pass over a medallion of the sun. I believe that everyone who visits our special place is welcomed and charged with a sliver of Brian's light. And when I say "charged with," I do mean that anyone in touch with Brian's life story is now held accountable in an energetic way to learn more, love better, or otherwise kick some ass in general.

Taking action and being of service to others is our legacy. I am lucky I had endless freedom to explore my professional passions, whether in IT, systems management, cutting hair, or helping people reach wellness goals that fueled bigger life accomplishments. In working on this book, which was initially meant to be a tribute to Brian, I heard a new call, one that feels like the culmination of everything I've experimented with so far. All the dots are connecting.

Thank you, Brian.

When you died and I slowed down, I learned to listen—I mean, I learned to really listen. I paid attention to our children in ways I had never realized I would have to or could. The skills I "gained" in exchange for such a loss hurt, and your death came at us so out of order, but it made me a better person. When I see that someone is stuck, afraid, not listening to what is possible for them because of grief or some other version of darkness and hell, I know that things will get better. Bad things happen to good people; we all fear risking and losing more than we already have risked and lost, but we can always take that first step of getting off the couch. We can turn woe into wonder. Rise up and fly in a new direction.

Thank you for sharing the time and space you shared with us.

We are lucky and we always will be.

❋

There are myriad options in every story—thousands of forks in the road, millions of revolving and sliding doors, billions of endings and beginnings. I've known some form of feeling stuck, feeling confused, or feeling foolish throughout my life, and I've been encouraged to practice "chilling" in the cage. So I'm not judging anyone. It's just that I see how making faith-fueled angel-assisted choices can help us push through pain to get to the kind of song that moves right through us.

What are you going to do between the chaos of living and the poetry of dying?

Most of my life, I believed the answer to my restlessness was to become an expert in one thing. That belief had me spinning in circles. Over and over I would get caught up in whatever new orbit started to pull at me, always hoping, "This is it! This is my life's purpose. From here on out, I'm set."

Life is never set, though, never fixed.

I exist right now to listen and then to guide people toward what could be, in the context of family. My gift is to help morphing, merging, rebirthing families as they learn how to fit together. I want each member of each family, community, or organization to shine their unique light on matters personal and universal, to open dialogue, and to be brave in the face of the complex challenges all of us—as one— are experiencing today. We need to effect change.

If other planes do exist, if the Irish Otherworld of Mag Argatnél is where Max went when he told me he'd found Brian in the underworld and talked to him, who am I to doubt it? This silver-cloud plain sounds like heaven to me, except I've always taken issue with the idea that heaven is a gated party we must demonstrate we are worthy of entering after we are dead. We have access to the joy, faith, and hope associated with the heavenly realm here and now. We have the capacity to generate and spread goodness and good energy on a daily basis. Some may say this is woo-woo or privilege or psychobabble, and in part this may be true. We don't *know*, though, so why not choose the story that is most life-affirming and strengthening for me and my family—for you and yours—for all others?

✹

Any leap from one reality to the next is possible, even if you have convinced yourself it's not and even when you have no idea what the next place, person, or version of your life will look like.

When I flew to Phoenix decades ago, my excitement for the bigger world was uncontainable. I cried, I met with like-minded service-oriented colleagues, and then I hiked, sweated, and marveled at the Praying Monk. Phoenix was the start of my journey toward an understanding that we are never alone and are never finished evolving and loving. We are the earthly lotus flower and the butterfly, as much as we are the phoenix of myth. We are scientist, entrepreneur, artist, spiritualist, poet, yogini, animal, practical—all in one and all one.

I've sometimes wondered while putting words to the page if I veer at all toward the overdramatic. In the eulogy I wrote for Brian, at his Celebration of Life services in Baltimore and Huntington Beach, I briefly felt the same concern. I asked audiences to consider the fact that they were living on borrowed time; I asked, "If you were to die tomorrow, could you be sure that you'd left nothing undone that you had wanted to do?"

My questions were sincere, and as time passes I know there is nothing melodramatic about them. The last lines of one of Mary Oliver's poems have been turned into a meme, printed out on inspirational wall posters, and repeated like a prayer over and over again by the multitudes of people who find her poems accessible, spiritual, and down-to-earth: "Tell me, what is it you plan to do with your one wild and precious life?"

You stand now at the forefront of an extensive legacy. What story are you writing?

Epilogue

At a keynote speech I had the privilege to give at the Governor's Utah Energy Summit of 2016, I invited the audience to sit back, relax, and take a deep breath.

I asked them these questions.

Are your affairs in order?

Does everyone you love KNOW that you love them?

Have you accomplished EVERYTHING you'd like to accomplish with your time here?

Have you had the kind of impact on your family, community, friends, and colleagues that makes you proud?

Those were some heavy questions to begin an energy conference with, but I asked them because I sincerely wanted each audience member to consider their legacy. I certainly hadn't given much thought to mine or to Brian's prior to December 22, 2011, but the evening I arrived to pick up my husband from the airport and was told that his plane didn't make it changed everything. At the age of thirty-eight, Brian Robertson died, and all we were left with was his legacy.

So I ask: If today were the last day of your life, what would people remember about you?